1500
INSPIRATIONAL
QUOTES
AND ILLUSTRATIONS

1500
INSPIRATIONAL
QUOTES
AND ILLUSTRATIONS

Compiled by the
M. Lunn Family

BAKER BOOK HOUSE
Grand Rapids, Michigan

Foreword

2923 Troost Avenue has been a familiar address to Nazarenes ever since 1926, when the Publishing House first occupied its permanent home there in the Beacon Hill section of Kansas City. Troost was a busy thoroughfare and its trolley line carried more passengers than any other in the city.

The situation was a "natural" for a wayside pulpit and M. Lunn, then manager of the House, seized the opportunity to set one up. It became the avenue by which this dedicated layman "preached" to thousands of people every day as he placed these short, pointed messages on the attractive board.

Collecting items for the "pulpit" intensified a hobby already established, and the Lunn scrapbook grew and grew. The family joined in, and in time the bulky volume contained over 1,500 items.

These gems, the product of 60 years of mining in a multitude of sources, are now being shared in this unique volume. Divided into more than 100 categories, alphabetically arranged, the material becomes readily accessible for whatever use it may have—even for a wayside pulpit! This is indeed a treasury of pithy thought, neatly turned phrases, and pungent truth.

—J. FRED PARKER
Book Editor

ABIDING

It is the dull, bald, dreary, commonplace day, with commonplace duties and people, that kills the burning heart unless we have learned the secret of abiding in Jesus.

—*Oswald Chambers*

ABSOLUTES

The four absolutes as taught by Oxford Group (later known as Moral rearmament) are: absolute honesty, absolute purity, absolute unselfishness, absolute love.

ACCOMPLISHMENTS

Success, achievement, fame, wealth: multiply earthly triumphs by a million, add them all together, and they are nothing—less than nothing, a positive impediment measured against one draught of that living water Christ offers to the spiritually thirsty, irrespective of who they are. What, I ask, does life hold? what is come which could possibly be put in the balance against the refreshment of drinking that water?

—*Malcolm Muggeridge*

◇   ◇   ◇

The world is full of great things to be accomplished: lawful things, necessary things, good things. Peter was doing a good thing, and so may I be, yet Jesus said to him, "Lovest thou me more than these?" and so may He say to me.

—*Charles A. McConnell*

◇   ◇   ◇

Take what you have, and make something of it.

—*E. Stanley Jones*

◇   ◇   ◇

"I might" may be waking up.
"I'll try" is on his feet.
"I can" is half done.
"I am doing it" is on the road to completion.
"I did it" is a success.

◇　◇　◇

No one is small who does a small job in a great way.

◇　◇　◇

Today's choices determine tomorrow's achievements.

◇　◇　◇

The man who does his job well needs no important ancestors.

◇　◇　◇

I divide the world into three classes: the few who make things happen; the many who watch things happen; and the overwhelming majority who have no notion of what happens.

—*Nicolas Murray Butler*

◇　◇　◇

Most of us can do more than we think we can, IF we would give ourselves the chance.

◇　◇　◇

The very best one can do is hard to beat.

◇　◇　◇

We cannot do everything at once, but we can do something at once.

—*Calvin Coolidge*

◇　◇　◇

Small deeds done are better than great deeds planned.

—*Peter Marshall*

◇　◇　◇

After all is said and done, more is said than done.

◇　◇　◇

There are three kinds of people in the world: the wills, the won'ts, and the can'ts. The first accomplish everything. The second oppose everything. The third fail in everything.

◇ ◇ ◇

No one ever does a worthwhile thing all by himself.

ACTIONS

What you are speaks so loudly I cannot hear what you say.

◇ ◇ ◇

Be what you wish others to become.

◇ ◇ ◇

Let yourself, and not your words, speak for you.

◇ ◇ ◇

The smallest good deed is better than the grandest good intention.

◇ ◇ ◇

One does evil enough when one does nothing good.

◇ ◇ ◇

Sometimes when we think twice, we do not act even once.

◇ ◇ ◇

You can preach a better sermon with your life than with your lips.

◇ ◇ ◇

The world will judge our doctrine by our deeds.

◇ ◇ ◇

A man's action is only a picture book of his creed.

◇ ◇ ◇

Don't forget to translate your words into deeds.

◇ ◇ ◇

Graven in marble, it perishes; written in deeds, it never dies.

◇ ◇ ◇

A thousand words will not leave so deep an impression as one deed.

◇   ◇   ◇

Our actions are our loudspeakers.

◇   ◇   ◇

Life is activity. Not singing about Christ tells the story of what He means in my life, but the sort of things I invest my energies in, and the spirit I show in day-by-day living. He is an everyday Saviour.

—*Bertha Munro*

◇   ◇   ◇

A Christian life is the exemplified version of the Bible.

◇   ◇   ◇

Do we demonstrate before the world what we confess? Is there anything about us and our movement that the world cannot explain away, about which it must say God is at work?

—*Leighton Ford*

◇   ◇   ◇

No good that we do is ever lost.

◇   ◇   ◇

Emotion is a poor substitute for action.

ALCOHOLISM

Think, and you won't drink.

◇   ◇   ◇

The odor of frying bacon goes a long way further toward making a happy home than does the odor of alcohol on the little wife's breath.

◇   ◇   ◇

The drunkard is a man who commits suicide on the installment plan.

AMBITION

The itching sensation that some people mistake for ambition is merely inflammation of the wishbone.

AMERICA

What America needs more than railway extension, western irrigation, a low tariff, a bigger cotton crop, and a larger wheat crop is a revival of religion, the kind that our fathers and mothers used to have—a religion that counted it good business to take time for family worship each morning right in the middle of harvest; a religion that made men quit work a half hour earlier on Wednesday so the whole family could get ready to go to prayer meeting.

—*"Wall Street Journal"*

◇　◇　◇

The English historian Arnold J. Toynbee made an unofficial fact-finding tour of the United States. Published in one of America's leading popular magazines was his rather dismal and distressing summary of a nation in crisis. Toynbee wrote of a nation that had lost the drive and optimism which a few short years ago had been its most apparent genius. He described a country in trouble around the world; and more importantly, a country in trouble with herself, threatened by domestic problems which might very well prove to be her undoing—disturbances on her campuses, riots in her cities, and disenchantment and distrust among her people.

—*Warren C. Hamby in "Winds of Change"* (Revell)

◇　◇　◇

The real world, the ugly, banal, godless religious world of America today!

◇　◇　◇

11

The Church is the bulwark of democracy. Strengthen it!

◇ ◇ ◇

Our nation got a good start by trusting in the Word of God with faith and assurance. America has forgotten her foundational belief and prides herself on scientific achievement. We do not need outer space, but inner peace; not revolution, but revival; not moritoriums, but prayer; not political resistance, but a resistance of evil; not the writings of Dylan, Mao Tse-tung, Bertrand Russell, or Norman Mailer, but the writings of God-inspired men.

—William Goodman

◇ ◇ ◇

I don't know how long America will be here—as long as it is a servant of Jehovah, surely. After that it simply moves on the chessboard of history. We may have stronger guns than Russia, but we no longer have stronger goals. Not what we have in our hearts but only what we have in our hands is now our strength. If we are overpowered, we have nothing.

—Louis F. Evans

◇ ◇ ◇

We are witness to the decline and fall of the American Republic unless there is a change, deep down in the American people, a genuine crusade against self-indulgence, immorality, public and private. May Craig calls for every citizen to clean out weakness and selfishness and immorality of all types, and then to choose leaders who with strength and principle and intelligence will lead us to where we can have self-respect and the respect of others. Would we elect such a man if he campaigned on such a platform?

◇ ◇ ◇

The Bible is the Rock on which our republic stands.

◇ ◇ ◇

No man ought to take his politics so seriously that he is unable to laugh occasionally at his own party.

◇　◇　◇

What Americans need most is a sense of direction.

◇　◇　◇

Whatever makes men good Christians makes them good citizens.

—Daniel Webster

◇　◇　◇

God never bestows great benefits upon any nation without a purpose.

◇　◇　◇

Stalin said that religion is the opiate of America and of any Christian nation. He was wrong—prosperity is. C. S. Lewis said that years of prosperity are "excellent campaigning weather" for the devil. He went on to say, "Prosperity knits a man to the world. He feels that he is finding his place in it, while really it is finding its place in him."

◇　◇　◇

There are some old things that made this country. There is the old virtue of incorruptible service and honor in public office. There are the old virtues of economy in government, of self-reliance, thrift, and individual liberty. There are the old virtues of patriotism, real love of country, and willingness to sacrifice for it.

—Herbert Hoover

◇　◇　◇

President Herbert Hoover, in discussing morality, said that it is one of the more perplexing and controversial problems facing our nation: "Primarily, it is because of individual and collective cowardice on the part of our society. We do not have the courage to stand in conflict

13

with the mad rush for material wealth, indulgence and social prestige."

◇   ◇   ◇

"Back to God" in repentance true!
"Back to God" to serve Him anew!
"Back to God" to win others too!
America, "Back to God!"
                    —R. Judson Wilkins

◇   ◇   ◇

The spirit of liberty is the spirit of Him who, nearly 2,000 years ago, taught mankind that lesson it has never learned but has never quite forgotten: that there may be a Kingdom where the least shall be heard and considered side by side with the greatest.

◇   ◇   ◇

Is there tragedy ahead for our nation? How can we avoid it?
    —The teacher says that education is the way out.
    —The philosopher says that reason is the way out.
    —The militarist says that armed power is the way out.
    —The politician says that legislation is the way out.
    —The scientist says that technology is the way out.
    —But God says that repentance is the only way out.

◇   ◇   ◇

Is our prosperity leading us to God, or away from Him? The peril which the Hebrews faced is the peril which accompanies prosperity in every age. Moses warned: "Beware that thou forget not the Lord thy God, in not keeping his commandments, and his judgments, and his statutes . . . lest when thou hast eaten and art full, and hast built goodly houses, and dwelt therein; and when thy herds and thy flocks multiply, and thy silver and thy gold is multiplied, and all that thou hast is multiplied; then thine heart be lifted up, and thou forget the Lord thy God."

◇   ◇   ◇

14

God's judgments on the nation of Israel were severe. They departed from what they knew to be right and continually ignored God's warnings. "Righteousness exalteth a nation: but sin is a reproach to any people" (Prov. 14:34).

◇   ◇   ◇

It is my conviction that our nation stands in need of a complete spiritual renaissance; our destiny in the coming decade is likely to depend on this factor more than any other.

—Mark Hatfield

◇   ◇   ◇

"I have lived a long time," Franklin told the delegates to the Constitutional Convention, "and the longer I live, the more convincing proofs I see of this truth, that God governs in the affairs of men. If a sparrow cannot fall to the ground without His notice, is it probable that an empire can rise without His aid? We have been assured in the sacred writings that 'except the Lord build the house, they labour in vain that build it.' I firmly believe this, and I also believe that without His concurring aid, we shall succeed no better in this political building than the builders of Babel."

◇   ◇   ◇

God of our fathers, known of old,
Lord of our far-flung battle line,
Beneath whose awful Hand we hold
Dominion over palm and pine—
Lord God of Hosts, be with us yet,
Lest we forget—lest we forget!

—Rudyard Kipling

◇   ◇   ◇

Edward Gibbon in *The Decline and Fall of the Roman Empire* gives five reasons for the downfall of this powerful

15

nation: (1) Their rapid increase of divorce; (2) Their constant increase of taxation; (3) Their mad craze for pleasure; (4) Their building of gigantic armaments; (5) Their downgrading of vital religion. Is there a lesson, a warning, for us?

◇　◇　◇

If we abide by the principles taught in the Bible, our country will go on prospering and continue to prosper; but if we and our posterity neglect its instructions and authority, no man can tell how sudden a catastrophe may overwhelm and bury our glory in profound obscurity.

—Daniel Webster

◇　◇　◇

We have become a nation of idolaters. Our idolatry may not be as crude as that of the Israelites in Old Testament times, but it is just as destructive. The shrines of material wealth, military power, personal pleasure, prestige, and popularity are crowded with worshippers.

◇　◇　◇

The noblest patriot is one who exerts his influence to raise the life of the nation to the level of its privileges; to harmonize the practice of brotherhood with the principle of brotherhood; to guarantee to every citizen the right to life, liberty, and the pursuit of happiness.

—Oliver G. Wilson

◇　◇　◇

He serves his country best
Who lives pure lives and doeth righteous deeds,
And walks straight paths, however others stray,
And leaves his sons, an uttermost bequest,
A stainless record, which all men may read.

—Susan Coolidge

ANGER

A person can be measured by the size of the thing it takes to get his goat.

◇   ◇   ◇

To be angry with a weak person is proof that you are not very strong yourself.

◇   ◇   ◇

Very few people are capable of making an absolutely accurate statement while they are angry.

◇   ◇   ◇

Some people seem to think they have not spoken forcibly if they have not spoken angrily.

◇   ◇   ◇

A chip on the shoulder is merely dandruff from the wood higher up.

◇   ◇   ◇

Anger is only one letter short of danger.

APATHY

The attitudes of some church members remind me of an epitaph which read: "Don't bother me ever. I want to be dead for ever and ever."

◇   ◇   ◇

General Apathy still has a large army in his control.

◇   ◇   ◇

There is an irreconcilable conflict between good and evil in our lives, in our society, and in existence itself. And yet few of us have any real sense of conflict between the Christian faith and the surrounding world.

APOLOGY

If you're willing to . . .
Admit you're all wrong . . .

When you are, you're . . .
All right.

◇   ◇   ◇

You needn't feel you're crawling when you say, "I'm sorry."

APPRECIATION
An ounce of appreciation is worth a pound of pressure.

ASSURANCE
I am more convinced in my heart than I am in my experience that the view of life Christ came into the world to preach, and died to sanctify, remains as true and as valid as ever, and that all who care to, young and old, healthy and infirm, wise and foolish, educated and uneducated, may live thereby, finding in our troubled, confused world, as in all other circumstances and at all other times, an enlightenment and a serenity not otherwise attainable.

—Malcolm Muggeridge

◇   ◇   ◇

To be conscious that He is with us, and that His power is immediately available in all the areas of our life, is to have that assurance and confidence that we so sorely need, not only in the crises that may come to us, but also in the humdrum round of everyday living.

◇   ◇   ◇

These words were seen on a tomb in a church in Buford in the Cotswold, England: "Drive out fear from my heart, O my body. I believe that you shall appear before God in Christ; for he it is that sustains you and calls you to dwell with him. Laugh at the threats of disease, despise the blows of misfortune, care not for the dark grave and go

18

forward at Christ's summons. For Christ will be to each man a kingdom, a light, a life, and a crown."

◇   ◇   ◇

I have learned to place myself before God every day as a vessel to be filled with His Holy Spirit. He has filled me with the blessed assurance that He, as the everlasting God, has guaranteed His work in me.

—Andrew Murray

◇   ◇   ◇

Christian faith gives one a consciousness, an awareness of God—oneness, fellowship, communion, a sense of being comfortable in His presence; an assurance that all is well. "This is my Father's world."

◇   ◇   ◇

I heard no outward voices; I saw no external light or vision of any kind; there was no text of scripture brought to my mind; neither did I feel any exterior joy. I received a conviction or evidence in my soul whereby I was assured that my sins were forgiven for Christ's sake, and that I was accepted of God in the Beloved.

—Thomas Rutherford

ATTITUDE

If you want to be distressed—look within
            —defeated—look back.
            —distracted—look around.
            —dismayed—look before.
            —delivered—look to Christ.
            —delighted—look up!

◇   ◇   ◇

The attitude within is more important than the circumstances without.

BACKSLIDING

It's the water in the ship that sinks it.

◇   ◇   ◇

A spiritual sag means a letdown somewhere along the line.

◇   ◇   ◇

When men begin to save their skins they begin to lose their souls.

◇   ◇   ◇

People are not shaken by attacks on their faith; they degenerate only when they begin to believe the highest standards are not required.

◇   ◇   ◇

The urge to accommodate is Christian, but there is a point beyond which we cannot go if we are to retain our identity as the redeemed of Christ.

—Ernest T. Campbell

◇   ◇   ◇

It is our omissions that form the cloud which gradually shuts God out of our lives.

—Bertha Munro

◇   ◇   ◇

How far into the secular can the sacred be taken before it becomes secular itself? How far can a person go in indulging his prejudices before he must confess that he is unregenerate? How far back can a person backslide before he has parted company, perhaps eternally, with the community of God?

—William Gray

◇   ◇   ◇

Unless there is within us that which is above us, we shall soon yield to that which is about us. Solomon yielded to "the lust of the flesh, and the lust of the eyes, and the pride of life." With us it could be the spirit of the age with its

20

purse, pleasure, and power passions. John Wesley defined it as seeking satisfaction in visible things. Adam Clarke said, "The lust of the eyes is inordinate desires after finery of every kind, gaudy dress, splendid houses, superb furniture, trappings and decorations of all sorts." He continued, "The pride of life is hunting after honors, titles, and pedigrees; boasting of ancestry, family connections, great offices, honorable acquaintances, and the like."

◇　◇　◇

The Godward pull of the Holy Spirit must be met with response. The presence of God in our hearts must be cultivated. If neglected it withers and dies and we become stunted, stilted, nice, respectable, nominal professed Christians.

BELIEF

If you don't live it, you don't believe it.

◇　◇　◇

Belief is more than intellectual acceptance. It is wholehearted identification of self with the interests, ideals, and purposes of Christ.

◇　◇　◇

It is said that Phillips Brooks used to lean over the pulpit at Harvard and say to the students, "Young gentlemen, believe in God, and in the last analysis nothing will ever overcome you."

◇　◇　◇

Belief is not a passive, receiving, compromising agreement. Belief is active. It is reaching, exploring, conquering affirmation. It is not seeking shelter; it is a searching confrontation with reality. Belief remains unswayed by doubts of others, for it is the closest thing to truth that we have found.

21

THE BIBLE

As the sun is necessary to read a sundial, so the Holy Spirit must illumine the Word and reveal its meaning. When thus illumined, God speaks to us through His Word.

◊   ◊   ◊

We should KNOW it in the head; STOW it in the heart; SHOW it in the life; SOW it in the world.

—Quoted by *J. Sidlow Baxter in "Mark These Men"*

◊   ◊   ◊

A casual, perfunctory reading of the Bible is not enough; the Bible must live and throb and glow in my heart and mind.

◊   ◊   ◊

The Bible must be read with receptive heart and open mind; it must become part of me, living and glowing in my entire being.

◊   ◊   ◊

We do need an interpreter, an infallible teacher, a trustworthy guide, and the Interpreter of the inspired Word is the Spirit of Truth. The mere grammarian cannot find it. The controversialist cannot explain it. The critic knows not its secret. The carnal mind cannot perceive it. The natural man cannot possess it. The twice-born see. The anointed know. The Spirit that revealed illumines, and He that inspired, interprets.

—*Samuel Chadwick*

◊   ◊   ◊

As the Bible speaks to us our minds will be illuminated, our hearts will be set aflame; God's living Word will burn within, consuming indifference and apathy.

◊   ◊   ◊

I am sorry for the men who do not read the Bible every day;

22

I wonder why they deprive themselves of the strength and the pleasure.

—*Woodrow Wilson*

◇　◇　◇

In times of great trouble, like the present time, our forebears used to turn to the Bible. It may sound pretty square to say so, but it was not a bad idea.

—*Stewart Alsop*

◇　◇　◇

The Bible is alive because it is the Book of the Living God.

◇　◇　◇

Cultivate your love for the Bible; guard your seasons of private devotions with it; nourish and strengthen your spiritual life from it; cherish its promises; anchor your very soul in its assurance of eternal life.

◇　◇　◇

The Bible is the Word of God speaking to men. It is the Revelation of God to mankind. It has power to enlighten, to motivate, to transform. It is the one Book through which God reveals His plan and His will.

◇　◇　◇

The Bible is not merely another book; it is a Book alive.

◇　◇　◇

How desperately the world needs the comfort, the inspiration, the counsel, the guidance of God's Book! Indeed, how the world needs the Bible: its precepts, its promises, its panacea for the ills of the individual and of society!

◇　◇　◇

Don't forget the precious old Book, the Bible. Take it to services with you.

◇　◇　◇

Many possess the Bible; too few are possessed by it.

◇　◇　◇

A Bible in the hand is worth two on the shelf.

◇　◇　◇

Perplexed? Need guidance? Reach for the Bible.

◇　◇　◇

The greatest word in the Bible is *God*; the sweetest, *Love*; the tenderest, *Come*; the longest, *Eternity*; and the shortest, *Now*.

◇　◇　◇

The Bible is translatable into everyday living.

◇　◇　◇

Do you delight to meditate on God's Word?

◇　◇　◇

It is not always the one who defends the Bible most vigorously who reads it most carefully.

◇　◇　◇

It is a little dangerous to quote the Bible unless you know what the original Author really meant.

◇　◇　◇

The Bible does not need to be rewritten, but reread.

◇　◇　◇

Thank God for the open Bible—but when did you last open yours?

BIBLE STUDY

If all hours are to be in some degree God-conscious, some hours should be deliberately so.

◇　◇　◇

There isn't any use trying to shine unless we take time to fill our lamps.

◇　◇　◇

You can assist your Sunday school teacher by studying your lesson for next Sunday. Why not begin right now?

◇　◇　◇

24

Study the Bible to be wise. Practice it to be righteous.

◇　◇　◇

A Bible that is falling apart probably belongs to somebody who isn't.

◇　◇　◇

Daily commune with God through Bible study and prayer.

BITTERNESS

The difficulties of life are intended to make us better, not bitter.

◇　◇　◇

People of good taste never say bitter things.

◇　◇　◇

Sarcastic remarks only reveal to others the bitterness of your own heart.

◇　◇　◇

Do not blame the Creator for the harvest when you do the sowing.

◇　◇　◇

The remedy for wrongs is to forget them.

◇　◇　◇

Life is too short to remember slights, to dream of tomorrow, to put off Christ.

◇　◇　◇

A chip on the shoulder is about the heaviest load anyone can carry.

BLESSINGS

The blessing that is shared leaves the soul enriched.

BOASTING

The man who has a right to boast doesn't have to.

BOREDOM, DRUDGERY

Drudgery, routine, and the daily grind are the test of faith and commitment.

◇　◇　◇

Drudgery is the touchstone of character.

—Oswald Chambers

◇　◇　◇

Routine is God's way of saving us between our times of inspiration.

—Oswald Chambers

◇　◇　◇

A rut is a grave with the ends pushed out a little.

◇　◇　◇

Life bores only when it has no purpose.

BRETHREN

Live in love as brethren.

BUSYNESS

The most serious idleness of all is being busy with things that do not matter. William Cowper's prayer is a worthy petition for us all:

> *O God, defend me from the task*
> *Of dropping buckets into empty wells,*
> *And growing old in drawing nothing up.*

—W. T. Purkiser

◇　◇　◇

These things that we see and handle every day are not the real, lasting things. How busy we are with them; how buried in them! Heavenly realities exist unnoticed, unseen; one day we shall stand face-to-face with them and be astonished—or confounded.

—Bertha Munro in "Truth for Today"

◇　◇　◇

We can become so involved in Kingdom activities that we don't have time for the King.

◇ ◇ ◇

Busy souls have no time to be busybodies.

◇ ◇ ◇

Do not let your left hand know what your right hand is doing; but be sure that it is busy doing something.

◇ ◇ ◇

We do not always achieve most when we are the busiest.

◇ ◇ ◇

Never be too busy to be kind.

◇ ◇ ◇

If you are too busy to help your fellowman, you are too busy.

CHANGES

The greatest mistake is to resist change.

◇ ◇ ◇

Plain horse sense ought to tell us that anything that makes no change in the man who professes it makes no difference to God, either.

—*A. W. Tozer*

◇ ◇ ◇

A changeless Christ for a changing world!

◇ ◇ ◇

Everywhere Jesus went, changes took place: the laws of nature were suspended; the very elements obeyed His command when winds quieted and waves subsided; devils were subject to His orders; children were loved, women were honored, despised publicans (tax collectors) were treated as brothers; a fallen woman was rescued from a mob intent on stoning her, and was told to sin no more; illiterate fishermen were called to be His trusted followers; diseases of every kind were healed—even death was compelled to give up its victims at the sound of His command, or the touch of His hand!

CHARACTER

Temptation conquered is Christian character strengthened.

—Bertha Munro in "Truth for Today"

◇ ◇ ◇

No one is born naturally or supernaturally with mature character. One has to make character by right choices, decisions, by enduring, by testings, by overcoming temptation.

◇ ◇ ◇

Character is pretty much like window glass—when it is cracked, it is cracked both inside and out.

—Norman R. Oke

◇ ◇ ◇

To build character, do every day some one thing you would rather not do.

◇ ◇ ◇

Death takes what you have and leaves you what you are.

◇ ◇ ◇

Men show their character in nothing more clearly than in what they think laughable.

—Goethe

◇ ◇ ◇

Reputation is precious; character is priceless.

◇ ◇ ◇

Character is what a man is in the dark.

◇ ◇ ◇

A man never shows his own character more plainly than by the way he portrays another's.

◇ ◇ ◇

Character must be forged. It is never inherited.

◇   ◇   ◇

No one has ever accidentally become better than he set out to be.

◇   ◇   ◇

We live in the character home we build.

◇   ◇   ◇

You cannot build character with good intentions.

◇   ◇   ◇

Character is made by what you stand for and reputation by what you fall for.

◇   ◇   ◇

Character is developed by seeking to help, not by seeking help.

◇   ◇   ◇

To hold the friends you make is a real test of character.

◇   ◇   ◇

Any man is what he is when he is not being watched.

◇   ◇   ◇

The measure of a man's real character is what he would do if he knew he would never be found doing it.

◇   ◇   ◇

Character is not made in a crisis—it is only exhibited.

◇   ◇   ◇

I would rather have an occupation that would soil my hands than one that would soil my character.

CHARITY

What you give for the cause of charity in health is gold; what you give in sickness is silver; what you give after death is lead.

—*Old Jewish Proverb*

◇   ◇   ◇

Charity, alone, will never save the world.

◇ ◇ ◇

The charity that longs to publish itself ceases to be charity.

CHEERFULNESS

Cheerfulness oils the machinery of life.

◇ ◇ ◇

Look on the brighter side.

◇ ◇ ◇

The cheerful man will do more in the same time, and do it better, than the sad or sullen.

—Thomas Carlyle

◇ ◇ ◇

Cheerfulness, like muscles, can be developed by systematic use.

CHRISTIAN GROWTH

One reason why the devotional life of many Christians is so shallow is that they are immersed in immediacies.

◇ ◇ ◇

"God is able to make all grace abound," enabling us to manifest the spirit of Christ when under pressure. This isn't always automatic, nor instantaneous. After the crisis experience comes the growing process: "Add to your faith . . ."; "Giving all diligence." Growth in Christlikeness requires constant, careful effort; perseverance; day-by-day discipline; taking yourself in hand; a growing procedure; a training program.

◇ ◇ ◇

Dedication is a lifetime process in which a Christian forms the habit of consciously involving Jesus Christ in every event of every day of his life.

◇ ◇ ◇

30

Walk wholeheartedly in all the light you have. It is a slow and difficult process to replace moral fiber.

—*Bertha Munro*

◇   ◇   ◇

A growing Christian must have his roots in the life-giving waters of penitence. The cultivation of a penitential spirit is absolutely essential to spiritual progress.

—*W. F. Smalley*

◇   ◇   ◇

Every Christian ought to have spiritual depths that are beyond his vocabulary.

◇   ◇   ◇

Christian fruit must be borne on Christ-abiding branches.

◇   ◇   ◇

Daily renewal is the prescription for growth in Christian experience, and growth is necessary for spiritual health and life.

◇   ◇   ◇

A new life begins each day. The break of day lifts the curtain on a new life; a fresh page in the book of records; a day to grow, to learn, to seek, to strive, to achieve, to serve. Each day is a rung in the ladder by which we climb to heaven.

◇   ◇   ◇

He was a man obviously saved by the recurring surprise and daily wonder of Christ. To him Christ came with a new astonishment every morning, with a new amazement of love and grace every evening.

◇   ◇   ◇

Every morning lean thine arms upon the windowsill of heaven and gaze upon thy Lord. Then with this vision in thy heart, turn strong to meet the day.

◇   ◇   ◇

The Apostle Paul declared, "I do not frustrate the grace of God." How tragically we limit God by our lack of responsiveness and receptivity!

◊　◊　◊

God breaks in and interrupts our carefully laid plans for creature comforts. God disturbs our complacency, our self-satisfaction, and quickens our discontent with fleeting things of time.

◊　◊　◊

Our potential in spiritual matters is measured by the promises of God and our faith in them.

CHRISTIAN LIFE

Five ways in which Christ makes life worthwhile:
1. A conscience you can live with
2. A creed you can live by
3. A cause you can live for
4. A company you can live in
5. A consummation you can live toward

◊　◊　◊

The victorious life isn't all illumination and inspiration; there are times of no ecstasy, no elation, no exuberance, no thrill. Just slogging along with unwavering determination.

◊　◊　◊

The Christian life is lived by faith.

◊　◊　◊

Lives rooted in God are never uprooted.

◊　◊　◊

The Christian life lived has no regrets.

◊　◊　◊

To be single-minded toward God means that we view each area of life in new and different perspective. Our entire life—personal, home, business, social—our means, our service, our relationships, are ordered with eternal values in mind.

CHRISTIAN LIVING

The finest compliment that can be paid to a Christian is "You have enriched my life."

◇   ◇   ◇

Do you want Christ to represent you above as you represent Him below?

◇   ◇   ◇

Faith makes a Christian; life proves a Christian; trial confirms a Christian; death crowns a Christian.

◇   ◇   ◇

Are you more concerned about what "they all do" than about what you should do?

◇   ◇   ◇

The secret of a sweet and Christian life is to live by the day. It is the long stretches that tire us.

◇   ◇   ◇

To live like Christ should be the aim of every Christian

◇   ◇   ◇

Daily ask God for a scripture; ask God for a song; ask God for someone in need whom you can help.

◇   ◇   ◇

The man who walks with God always gets to his destination.

◇   ◇   ◇

All our days belong to God.

◇   ◇   ◇

Christ taught that it is better to accept evil than to inflict it.

◇   ◇   ◇

Two are blessed when your radiant spirit shines on another's gloom.

◇ ◇ ◇

Christ died for you; are you living for Him?

◇ ◇ ◇

Keep sunshine on your face, honey on your tongue, and Christ in your heart.

◇ ◇ ◇

Kindness in little things is a Christian virtue.

◇ ◇ ◇

Even those who cannot understand our theology can understand our Christian kindliness.

◇ ◇ ◇

If we let God guide, He will provide.

◇ ◇ ◇

The sun shines brightest above the fog. On gloomy days, climb!

◇ ◇ ◇

Do what you can, where you are, with what you have.

◇ ◇ ◇

Be patient; keep sweet; do not fret; do your best; and leave the results with God.

◇ ◇ ◇

Christian walk must keep step with Christian talk.

◇ ◇ ◇

Some people are content to spend a weekend with Jesus, but balk at having Him as a permanent Guest in their homes.

◇ ◇ ◇

It is not well for a man to pray cream and live skim milk.

—*Henry Ward Beecher*

◇ ◇ ◇

The law of moral gravitation pulls a man toward what he loves.

◇ ◇ ◇

If a man cannot be a Christian in the place he is, he cannot be a Christian anywhere.
—*Henry Ward Beecher*

◇ ◇ ◇

Strive always to be like a good watch: open-faced, busy hands, pure gold, well regulated, full of good works.

◇ ◇ ◇

We either walk forward, fall back, or take root.

◇ ◇ ◇

Live carefully; the soul you save may be your own.

◇ ◇ ◇

Practice makes perfect—especially the practice of what we preach.

◇ ◇ ◇

There are no detour signs along the straight and narrow path.

◇ ◇ ◇

Consistent Christians always command respect.

◇ ◇ ◇

Lord, give me appreciation of my limitations; let me know the responsibility of my high calling; let me show forth Thy love!

◇ ◇ ◇

W-ords
A-ctions
T-houghts
C-ompany
H-eart

◇ ◇ ◇

Practice in life whatever you pray for.

◇   ◇   ◇

Never do what you can't ask Christ to bless, and never go
to any place that you cannot ask Christ to go with you.

◇   ◇   ◇

The little word *ALL* is significant: all your care; all your
time; all your purpose.

◇   ◇   ◇

If we do not have causes, hopes, purposes, understandings
of life to which we are devoted because we are Christians—
causes in which many people and much of the common
way of life do not believe—we are missing the way.

◇   ◇   ◇

Keep us, O God, from pettiness. Let us be large in thought,
in word, in deed.

◇   ◇   ◇

As thou art in church or cell, that same frame of mind
carry out into the world, into its turmoil and its fitfulness.

◇   ◇   ◇

If God is really central, then our time, our pleasures, our
relationships with others, our most humdrum tasks are
gathered up and offered as of far more value than
calves, or rams, or ten thousand rivers of oil.

—Leslie D. Weatherhead

◇   ◇   ◇

We ought daily to renew our vows and to kindle our hearts
to zeal, as if each day were the first day of our conversion,
and to say, "Help me, O God, in my good resolutions
and in Thy holy service, and grant that this day I may
make a good beginning, for hitherto I have done nothing."

—Thomas a Kempis

◇   ◇   ◇

A practicing Christian involves his faith in every aspect of life, every day.

◇ ◇ ◇

Are you a practicing Christian? If so, every single act and feeling, every experience, whether pleasant or unpleasant, must be referred to God. It means looking at everything as something coming from Him, and always looking to Him and asking His will first, and saying: "How would He wish me to deal with this?"

◇ ◇ ◇

Every day can be alive with the thrill of romance if we will live it fresh with God.

—*Bertha Munro in "Truth for Today"*

◇ ◇ ◇

In difficult times, does our Christianity give us a substantial faith to lean on? When days are dark, does it restore our hope and enable us to set our affections on things above? In hours of personal anguish and distress, does it bring to us the touch of healing? In moods of resentment over wrongs done, does it mellow our antagonism and restore our poise? It must do all that and more. It must give us self-mastery.

◇ ◇ ◇

A mind through which Christ thinks;
A heart through which Christ loves;
A voice through which Christ speaks;
A hand through which Christ uplifts.

◇ ◇ ◇

Some things, some of our good things, are not wrong, but we have neither time nor energy for them if we would invest heavily in Christ-fellowship.

◇ ◇ ◇

Christ took on our human nature that we might partake of His divine nature. So we react to opposition, difficult

37

circumstances, hard days, unpleasant situations, tough times, annoyances, peculiar people with fortitude, submission, not by our human nature, but by God's nature.

CHRISTIAN STAND

Abraham did not "adjust to his environment." He and God made a new environment wherever he went. Try it! Christians are not called to conform; they are called to convict.

—Bertha Munro in "Truth for Today"

◇　◇　◇

The Early Church had a simple creed: "Jesus Christ is Lord."

◇　◇　◇

Some people stand for nothing because they fall for everything.

CHRISTIANITY

Every group, however Christianized, proceeds upon a pilgrimage from which the human element cannot be removed.

—Robert A. Williams

◇　◇　◇

Christianity is not belief in an idea; it is not being connected to an institution; it is love and commitment to a Person. To be a Christian an individual gives everything he knows of himself to everything he knows of Jesus Christ.

—W. Robert Smith

◇　◇　◇

Vital Christianity presupposes:
　　—an open mind which allows God to speak His message

—an open heart which allows the melting, molding work of the Holy Spirit

—An open Bible which allows God's will and purposes to be made known

◇ ◇ ◇

Christianity js not subscribing to a creed; it is loving attachment to a Person.

◇ ◇ ◇

The disciplined scholar is Christianity's intellectual defense, but it is the delivered sinner who constitutes Christianity's practical defense.

◇ ◇ ◇

It is impossible to be a Christian unless God has in some measure revealed himself to us in the person of Jesus Christ.

◇ ◇ ◇

A man is a Christian in all his ways, or he is not a Christian.

◇ ◇ ◇

Who is qualified to be termed a Christian? Anyone who responds affirmatively to Jesus Christ. P. Carnegie Stepson writes: "A Christian is anyone who is responding to whatever meanings of Christ are, through God's Spirit, being brought home to his intellectual or moral conscience. This is a definition at once exhaustive of the profoundest Christianity and admissive of the simplest."

◇ ◇ ◇

Being a Christian does not consist of holding belief *A*, plus belief *B*, plus belief *C*, and so on. It consists in living in a deeply personal relationship of trust and obedience with God. This relationship is the mold out of which Christian beliefs grow and within which they are nourished.

—Charles S. Duthie

◇ ◇ ◇

The Christian word *parish* comes from a Greek word meaning "a body of aliens in the midst of any community." "I beseech you as aliens or exiles" (1 Pet. 2:11).

◇　◇　◇

All other faiths are philosophies or moralisms—a man's search upward. The gospel is God's search downward. Religions are man's search for God. The gospel is God's search for man. There are many religions, but only one gospel.

—*E. Stanley Jones*

◇　◇　◇

What makes the Christian belief different? It is a personal God who loves, cares, forgives: who makes himself known to us; who communicates.

◇　◇　◇

Christianity is not a seventh-day religion, but it is a religion for seven days.

◇　◇　◇

Christianity is equal to any task it has to perform.

◇　◇　◇

Christianity is *the answer,* not *an* answer, to the problems of today.

◇　◇　◇

Christianity is not a theory; it is an experience.

◇　◇　◇

Christianity is not a new leaf; it is a new life.

◇　◇　◇

Christianity has been the mother of all modern education.

◇　◇　◇

Real Christianity is always contagious.

◇　◇　◇

Christianity is not an insurance policy, but a call to arms.

CHRISTMAS

We are in danger of losing the awe, the wonder, the praise of true worship by failing to keep before us constantly the mystery and glory of the Incarnation.

—William Greathouse

◇   ◇   ◇

To the extent that our faith gets away from Jesus as God come down to us, we forget what Christianity really is. Our religion becomes just a moral code and a ritual when we lose the wonder of Jesus Christ. And that wonder is that He was truly God, and truly man.

◇   ◇   ◇

Wise men still seek Him.

◇   ◇   ◇

The glorious truth of the Incarnation is that Jesus comes into our human situation from God, entering all the way into our desperate sin and need, becoming fully man.

◇   ◇   ◇

When you take a cup of water from an ocean, or even a barrel of water, you no longer have an ocean. But when you take Deity in the form of a Babe in a manger, you still have God.

◇   ◇   ◇

Let's approach Christmas with an expectant hush, rather than a last-minute rush.

◇   ◇   ◇

If Jesus had not come, there would be no good tidings, no carols, no joy, no peace, no security, no Saviour!

◇   ◇ . ◇

In Denmark people say to one another at Christmastime, "May God bless your Christmas and may it last until Easter." That's a whole lot better than our jolly "Merry Christmas," isn't it!

◇   ◇   ◇

41

It is not Christmas without Christ.

◇   ◇   ◇

Let's put Christ into Christmas.

◇   ◇   ◇

The three wise men saw the light and followed it. They are rightly called wise!

◇   ◇   ◇

He who has no Christmas in his heart will never find one under a tree.

◇   ◇   ◇

You, too, may hear the angels' song—if you tune in!

◇   ◇   ◇

Jesus came to make the world over.
It was an old world and He came to make it new;
It was a tired world and He came to give it rest;
It was a sorrowing world and He came to bid it rejoice;
It was a dark world and He came to give it light;
It was a dying world and He came to give it life;
It was an imprisoned world and He came to give it liberty;
It was a lost world and He came to take it back to God.

THE CHURCH

Each one of us is the Church inside a small circle.

◇   ◇   ◇

The strength of the Church lies in the number of her first-line combat troops.

◇   ◇   ◇

No teacher can make scholars out of truants; no army can win a war with deserters; the church is both a school and an army, and cannot do its work with those who never attend.

◇   ◇   ◇

The church ceases to be a spiritual society when it is on the lookout for the development of its own organization.

—*Oswald Chambers*

◇   ◇   ◇

Jesus never said, "My home," or, "My wife," or, "My child"; but He did say, "My church."

◇   ◇   ◇

The universal body of Christ, made up of Blood-washed believers in every communion, and not to be identified with any local or denominational body, is the Lord's Church.

◇   ◇   ◇

Christ died for the Church. Anything worth dying for is worth saving. This is what God has called us to do: to save and build the Church, for which Christ gave His life.

—*James Hamilton*

◇   ◇   ◇

The Church's whispers must become her shouts; her lethargy must become enthusiasm; and her subdued light must become a beacon set upon the hilltops of the world.

—*Lester DeKoster*

◇   ◇   ◇

The Church has no right to be imperfect—it simply isn't entitled to that luxury; the world needs it too much.

—*Wesley C. Baker*

◇   ◇   ◇

Out of the church must go forth vigorous, healthy men and women who went in maimed and paralyzed. Broken things that no one could mend have been made whole again.

—*John Henry Jowett*

◇   ◇   ◇

The sacraments of the church often become almost a fetish, and the result is a cold, lifeless church. What a travesty on Christianity when compared with the early believers who with flaming hearts and a burning testimony of Christ marched triumphant amid their sufferings from nation to nation.

—*H. M. Shuman*

◇　◇　◇

The presence of a mother makes a home. The presence of a king makes a royal court. The presence of Christ makes a church.

◇　◇　◇

The chief counts in the indictment against the Church are three in number: worldliness, unbrotherliness, and indifference.

—*J. Fred Parker*

◇　◇　◇

The world at its worst calls for the Church at its best.

◇　◇　◇

In its passion for the pleasant the Church may lose its terribleness. God forbid. Men should have a great quaking fall upon them by reason of our divine vision.

—*Dinsdale T. Young*

◇　◇　◇

When the fire of spiritual devotion goes out, ritualism finds its opportunity. Aids to voluptuous meditation take the place of reverent adoration. If there be no power to cast out devils, transform sinners, and save souls, there are other ministries within reach.

—*Samuel Chadwick*

◇　◇　◇

The atmosphere of the Apostolic Church is charged with divine power. Their word was with power. Conviction accompanied their speech. Signs and wonders confirmed their testimony. They uncovered the hearts of evildoers, and heaven put its seal upon their judgments. Rulers trembled in their presence. The dead heard their voice. Disease fled at their touch. Devils were subject to their word. The presence of the Spirit endued man with divine authority and power. . . . The normal life of the Church was filled, inspired, and empowered in the fullness of the Spirit of the living God.

—*Samuel Chadwick*

◇　◇　◇

A live church is seeking out sinners; the real calamity for a church occurs when it becomes full of "nice" people on a "nice" street in a "nice" neighborhood. A nice little church can never be of much use in the work of the kingdom of God.

—*Halford Luccock*

◇　◇　◇

The farther any institution moves away from essentials and the high purpose for which it was founded, the more attention and importance it places upon incidentals. Let us beware of becoming prisoners of the unimportant.

◇　◇　◇

Soul-saving religion touches the spirit and genius of man. It burns in the soul. It is contagious. Others catch its glow and warmth. But the fire can burn low and even go out. This is a personal matter. A church is made up of individuals and each must ask himself if he is a spiritually dynamic person. Soul passion is a mighty force in the realm of religion. A church spiritually alive, moved by the presence of God, possesses great inner resources. Such a church is sufficient in itself and men who contact it will feel the holy dynamic.

◇　◇　◇

When religion turns to humanity for its inspiration and

to the world for its power, God is dethroned and the sanctuary becomes a secularized fellowship.

—*Samuel Chadwick*

◇　◇　◇

The church can get along without us, but we cannot get along without the church.

—*Richard S. Taylor*

◇　◇　◇

The church can become a museum for the preservation of hallowed traditions and institutions, doctrines, and sentiment. In that case it has no life; it has lost its driving force.

◇　◇　◇

The church is a workshop, not a dormitory.

◇　◇　◇

There are three growing gaps in the Church's relationship with the world: a credibility gap, a relevance gap, and a performance gap.

◇　◇　◇

Vitality was the chief, the outstanding characteristic of the Early Church. Such vitality is opposed to mere form, to a ritual or program of routine, lifeless repetition.

◇　◇　◇

The church is on the stretch for new methods, new plans, new buildings, new organizations. God is looking for better men. The Holy Ghost does not come upon methods, but upon men.

—*Samuel Chadwick*

◇　◇　◇

Pews are built to stand as regular use as pulpit chairs.

◇　◇　◇

Informality is not evidence of piety nor is a scorn of forms proof of exalted spirituality.

—*Charles Jefferson*

◇　◇　◇

You don't need an excuse for going to church.

◇   ◇   ◇

The surest way toward peace and happiness is by way of the church steps.

◇   ◇   ◇

No one can fill your pew for you.

◇   ◇   ◇

No dashing rain can make us stay
When we have tickets for the play.
But if a drop the walk besmirch,
Then it's too wet to go to church.

◇   ◇   ◇

There are two kinds of people in our churches: pillars and caterpillars. The pillars hold up the church while the caterpillars go in and out.

◇   ◇   ◇

Some families must think the Sunday service is like a convention: they just send one delegate.

◇   ◇   ◇

Too many people become a part of the membership without becoming a part of the fellowship.

◇   ◇   ◇

If people used the same excuses on the job that they use toward church they would be telling the boss there are too many hyopcrites working for him, so they think they will quit.

◇   ◇   ◇

Too many people are trying to thumb their way to heaven by joining a church.

◇   ◇   ◇

Church members are somewhat like mules; they cannot kick and pull at the same time.

◇   ◇   ◇

Be sure the church service is never helped by your absence.

◇　◇　◇

The church is fairly well supplied with conductors. It shows a shortage of engineers. But there is an oversupply of brakemen.

◇　◇　◇

As a church member are you portraying Christ, or betraying Him?

◇　◇　◇

A good investment is time spent in God's house.

◇　◇　◇

Folks who find the church cold usually sit on the back seat near the door.

◇　◇　◇

The duty of the whole congregation should not be the task of just a few.

◇　◇　◇

The difference between listening to a radio sermon and going to church is the same as the difference between calling your girl on the telephone and spending an evening with her.

◇　◇　◇

The best people on earth will be in church next Sunday.

◇　◇　◇

The test of a church is not the kind of people it attracts, but the kind of people it produces.

◇　◇　◇

The church that is not training its people to pray is not preparing them for the days that are ahead.

◇　◇　◇

The church is at ease when its people are more concerned with machinery than with men and women, with their structures of organization than they are with their mission in the world.

—*W. T. Purkiser*

◇　◇　◇

Too often the church program appeals largely to the carnal man in order to create interest and enthusiasm. To be able to apprehend God through the truth and by pure faith is the way of true progress.

—*H. M. Shuman*

◇　◇　◇

We may well be alarmed by noting the loss of peculiar value which comes to all enlarging institutions!

—*C. H. Zahniser*

◇　◇　◇

The greatest drag on Christianity today, the most serious menace to the Church's mission, is not the secularism without; it is the reduced Christianity within.

—*James S. Stewart*

◇　◇　◇

A scoffer characterized the church as a place of soft music, soft pews, and soft soap.

◇　◇　◇

It is dangerous and inexcusable rationalization to let ourselves think that spirituality is imperishable in any denomination, including our own.

◇　◇　◇

The first steps toward the better life are the church steps.

◇　◇　◇

It takes more than money to support a church!

CLOSED DOORS

When there seems to be no way out, look up.

◇　◇　◇

When God shuts a door, He opens a window.

◇ ◇ ◇

When one door closes, God opens another.

◇ ◇ ◇

One of God's favorite ways of revealing His will is by closing doors.

◇ ◇ ◇

Stops, as well as steps, are ordered by the Lord.

COMMITMENT

The channels between our souls and God get clogged by disobedience, neglect, by withholding or failing to keep committed. The channel is kept open by daily renewal, by having our hearts cleansed daily from wrong attitudes toward others.

◇ ◇ ◇

The great word of Jesus to His disciples is "abandon."

—*Oswald Chambers*

◇ ◇ ◇

God doesn't trust the dynamic of His power to the man of mixed motives. It is the committed, the dedicated, the fully consecrated man, the man with singleness of purpose whom God uses; the man who can say with the Apostle Paul, "For to me to live is Christ."

◇ ◇ ◇

Let God have your life. He can do more with it than you can!

◇ ◇ ◇

He who offers God a second place offers Him no place.

—*John Ruskin*

◇ ◇ ◇

Christ won't be anything to you unless He is everything.

◇ ◇ ◇

Give God a chance:
   —by believing,
   —by tithing,
   —by praying,
   —by obeying,
   —by yielding.

◇   ◇   ◇

God can give himself to us only in the measure in which we give ourselves to Him.

◇   ◇   ◇

The life of faith starts when you give yourself—yield, submit, surrender. Then you are in God's hands. You are on God's side. You have made a choice. Your will has rejected one way of life and accepted another.

◇   ◇   ◇

Never say no to God.

◇   ◇   ◇

If any man really desires to go right, the way will surely open.

◇   ◇   ◇

Line up on God's side. He has the power. Put your trust, your confidence in Him. Do this and someday you will stand at the end of time in the dawning of eternity and look back over the whole sweep of God's leadings in your life. Then you will see how sure, how safe you were in putting your whole trust in Him.

◇   ◇   ◇

To be a Christian means a total break with the past.

◇   ◇   ◇

Yielding to Christ is confessing every known sin in your life, yielding every area of your life. It means yielding your girl friend, your boyfriend, your family, your business, your career, your ambitions, your soul, the innermost thoughts and depths of your heart; yielding them all to Christ, holding nothing back.

—*Billy Graham*

◇　◇　◇

There are those who have gone only halfway in their acceptance of Christ. They have accepted Christ's cross, but not their own. Christ is their Saviour, they say, but He is not their Lord. A partial Christianity is a vicious thing. It comes from an attempt to have a half-Christ. Can Christ be divided?

◇　◇　◇

Each of us is continually bombarded by pressures—some complex, some simple—to establish material rather than spiritual standards as controlling influences in our lives. Establishing Christ as Lord of our lives is sometimes a struggle because of opposing forces. The pull, the gravitation, of earthly interests must be nullified by the upward pull of eternal values. The magnetism of "that which I cannot lose" should exercise a power which helps me to evaluate and discard "that which I cannot keep."

◇　◇　◇

The extent of our commitment determines our worth to the kingdom of God.

◇　◇　◇

We do not take God and His way seriously enough. We want God's way in a nice, quiet, genteel, inoffensive way that will not ruffle the opposition or unduly disturb our calm. We shrink from paying the full price.

◇　◇　◇

If we are to live and move and have our being in God, there must be reckless abandonment to Him.

◇　◇　◇

You cannot consecrate what is not yours. There is only one

52

thing you can consecrate to God, and that is the right to yourself.

—*Oswald Chambers*

◇　◇　◇

The biggest and hardest step to take in the process of becoming Christlike, or in reflecting Christ in your life at home, socially, in business, is submitting, yielding to God.

COMMON SENSE
Dollars will do better if they are accompanied by common sense.

COMPASSION
Everyone you meet is fighting a tough battle!

◇　◇　◇

The one who stops to lift another's load soon finds that he has lightened his own.

◇　◇　◇

A loving word may heal and bless.

◇　◇　◇

To pity distress is but human; to relieve it is Godlike.

COMPLAINING
I grumbled because I had to get up early in the morning—until one morning when I couldn't get up.

◇　◇　◇

Putting your best foot forward doesn't mean to kick about everything!

◇　◇　◇

If we could buy happiness we would probably be unhappy about the price.

◇　◇　◇

He who kicks continually soon loses his balance.

◇　◇　◇

Chronic bellyaching is nothing more than a bid for sympathy or attention.

◇　◇　◇

When you are pulling you have no time to kick, and when you are kicking you have no time to pull.

◇　◇　◇

Those with the most horse sense do the least kicking.

◇　◇　◇

Those who are constantly kicking rarely have a leg to stand on.

◇　◇　◇

No talent, no self-denial, no brains, no character is required to set up in the grumbling business.

◇　◇　◇

Learn to stop grumbling. If it is bad, keep it to yourself.

◇　◇　◇

It pays to close the book of complaints and open the book of praise.

CONCERN

He who makes no effort has no concern.

◇　◇　◇

When a Christian is not concerned about the salvation of others, he should be concerned about his own.

CONCEIT

The fellow with an inflated opinion of himself will one day wake up and find himself a flat tire.

◇　◇　◇

A man wrapped up in himself makes a small package.

◇   ◇   ◇

An egotist: One who is always me-deep in conversation.

◇   ◇   ◇

Those who sing their own praises seldom receive an encore.

◇   ◇   ◇

Superficial people like to be at the head of the parade.

◇   ◇   ◇

He who imagines he can do without the world deceives himself much; but he who fancies that the world cannot do without him is still more mistaken.

◇   ◇   ◇

The fellows who toot their own horns not only annoy others; they soon run down their own batteries.

◇   ◇   ◇

He who falls in love with himself will find no rival.

◇   ◇   ◇

Want a remedy for conceit? Think of all the things you *don't* know.

CONDUCT
Conduct is character in action.

◇   ◇   ◇

Jesus is always at the mercy of our misbehavior.

◇   ◇   ◇

There is no right way to do a wrong thing.

◇   ◇   ◇

There is only one man that can be responsible for my conduct, and that is myself.

—Henry J. Cadbury

◇   ◇   ◇

Be such a person and live such a life that if every person were such as you, and every life like yours, this earth would be God's paradise.

CONCILIATION
It is amazing how many times a delicate situation can be straightened out by talking it over with the other party.

◇　◇　◇

Build bridges instead of walls.

◇　◇　◇

Reconciliation begins when one party makes the first move.

CONFORMITY
It is always easier to go with the crowd than to battle your way against it. It is always easier to conform than to be a nonconformist.

—*William Barclay*

◇　◇　◇

One of the pitfalls of easygoing tolerance is neutrality.

—*Bernard T. Lowman*

◇　◇　◇

They who always follow the crowd finally become a part of it.

◇　◇　◇

The converse of transformation is conformation, which is taking on the shape of our surroundings. Rom. 12:2 speaks of being transformed "by the renewing of your mind." The Greek word for *renewal* suggests "keeping alive at the center."

◇　◇　◇

So often we are strict about things that don't matter, and so insensitive to the things that do! It is easy to accent the secondary, the trivial, the marginal, the transient, and overlook things of vital import and eternal worth.

◇   ◇   ◇

No dedicated Christian has to compromise his convictions in order to "make the best of both worlds."

◇   ◇   ◇

A certain book stated that it is the function of religion "to make a man feel at home in the world." False! A man can make himself so comfortably at home in the world about him that it becomes his whole universe and he forgets the spiritual world to which he belongs.

◇   ◇   ◇

The devil suggests, Don't reject the gospel; reduce it.

◇   ◇   ◇

A sure sign of spiritual declension is to make a practice of conformity and compromise, of comfort and opportunism, of unwillingness to venture for the good and to take a stand, of unwillingness to be different, of wanting to be good and religious but not too good and not too religious.

CONSCIENCE

In 1811 the United States Government established a "Conscience Fund." In excess of $3 million has been paid into that fund.

◇   ◇   ◇

There is no better health preservation than a clear conscience.

◇   ◇   ◇

Quite often when a man thinks his mind is getting broader it is only his conscience stretching.

◇   ◇   ◇

Every man makes his conscience either the prosecuting attorney or the lawyer for the defense.

◇   ◇   ◇

Envy no man who lives with a guilty conscience.

◇ ◇ ◇

He will easily be content and at peace whose conscience is pure.

◇ ◇ ◇

A clear conscience is a soft pillow.

CONTEMPORARY SCENE

This is the age
Of the half-read page.
And the quick hash
And the mad dash.
The bright night
With the nerves tight.
The plane hop
With the brief stop.
The lamp tan
In a short span.
The Big Shot
In a good spot.
And the brain strain
And the heart pain.
And the catnaps
Till the spring snaps—
And the fun's done.

—*Virginia Brasier in "Saturday Evening Post"*

◇ ◇ ◇

Nothing can save a tottering civilization but a towering Saviour.

—*Paul Rees*

◇ ◇ ◇

Every age has its own typical malady. Ours is a neurosis brought on by an amoral civilization, a materialism, a

58

misplaced humanism, an irresolution, a lack of conviction.

◇   ◇   ◇

A generation ago Dean Inge said, "The future belongs to the nations with a lower standard of living and a higher standard of work than ours." The disciplined receive the trophies, the indulgent get the consequences.

—Arnold E. Airhart

◇   ◇   ◇

Man struggles under three tyrannies: ego, things, people. We tend to be self-centered, materialistic, crowd-followers.

◇   ◇   ◇

Tell the social welfare people that it isn't enough to change an underprivileged person's environment, to feed him and clothe him. Man must be born anew, made a new creature. No one yet has had money enough, nor brains enough, nor a program effective enough to change the leopard's spots of sin.

◇   ◇   ◇

Day by day people, especially our young people, are bombarded with stimulation of desires that require no stimulation.

—William S. Banowsky in "It's a Playboy World"

◇   ◇   ◇

One of the fallacies of the twentieth century is that the moral character of a nation as a whole can be better than that of its citizens as individuals.

◇   ◇   ◇

How insensitive we can become to real values! How easily we are impressed by things which will be unimportant and insignificant in a few years!

◇   ◇   ◇

There's a lamentable lack of heartfelt religion today. Sure, there is no dearth of historic faith, of head knowledge of religion. Many give intellectual assent to God and the gospel, but their hearts, the affections, are directed toward material things of this world. "Where your treasure is, there will your heart be also."

◇ ◇ ◇

Wrong or right depends upon principle involved, not on what is expedient or humanly reasonable at the moment. That rules out situation ethics. Truth, righteousness, are basic, relevant, inexorable, unrelenting in individual life, in the church, in national affairs. They cannot be changed by persuasion or entreaty.

◇ ◇ ◇

Our humanity is trapped by moral adolescents. We have too many men of science, too few men of God. The world has achieved brilliance without wisdom, and power without conscience.

—*Omar Bradley*

◇ ◇ ◇

When Stanley found Livingstone in the African jungle, one of the first questions the latter asked was, "How is the world getting along?" Over the hearts and minds of multitudes of people today that question hovers like a great, dark cloud: "How is the world getting along?" As one writer put it, "Above us the constant threat of war so awful, so universal, so destructive as would lay the planet waste in horror. Around us millions who are permanently hungry; millions who are slaves in labor camps or prisons; slums, destitution, frustration, and appalling evil." Only God can save us from all this!

◇ ◇ ◇

Two-thirds of the world's population is always hungry. Every day 200,000 people die of starvation or deficiency disease. In India alone 50 million children will die of malnutrition in the next 10 years. More than half the world's 3.2 billion people live in perpetual hunger. Twenty million people in South Korea live 500 to a square mile, and only one acre in three yields food. Thirty-five million refugees are homeless upon the face of the earth today!

◇　◇　◇

Modern western society is dominated and governed by noise, newspapers, radio, and speed, so that men have lost the sense of inner meditation, of mature reflection, and thoughtful action. But all of this feverish activity is also a form of flight, by means of which men are trying to cover up the unease in their hearts, their spiritual emptiness, their defeats, and their rebellion.

—Paul Tournier, M.D.

◇　◇　◇

A psychiatrist says that 75 percent of all the people who go to the Mayo Clinic have nothing organically wrong with them.

◇　◇　◇

A world of cleverness without compassion, wit without humor, passion without values, of fantasy unredeemed by faith.

—David H. C. Read

◇　◇　◇

This is an age of dry eyes, hard noses, and cold feet. It follows the wind; it embraces the darkness; it loves a vacuum. Its beatitude is, "Blessed are the smooth, for they shall never be wrinkled."

◇　◇　◇

Behind the remarkably placid masks of the faces we see every day on the streets and in our businesses and clubs there lies a world of twisting souls, living with frustration and the fear of failure and meaninglessness, a world of souls without rudders, without any real sense of ultimate direction.

—*Keith Miller*

◇　◇　◇

Few would deny that there is a vast uneasiness abroad in the world. Christ's incisive phrase "men's hearts failing them for fear" is vividly descriptive of our day.

The symptoms of our collective disease are many and varied. There is little need to go over the sorry list again. The planless, day-to-day, fatalistic attitude toward life; the erosion of moral integrity on a mass scale; the loss of modesty and common decency, the debasing and commercialization of sex; the challenge to all organized human life posed by violence, crime, delinquency, class, and mass hatred—these are just a random sampling of signs of the sickness of society.

—*W. T. Purkiser*

◇　◇　◇

What's wrong with the world? The men themselves,
　Just men and their willful wills;
They make their customs and write their laws,
　But they cannot cure their ills.

—*Annie Johnson Flint*

◇　◇　◇

Perhaps the dominant characteristic of a despairing world is that it is a world where there are no absolutes, no stationary lighthouses by which man may steer in his perilous voyage. This is particularly true of moral values.

◇　◇　◇

This is the age of grown men wrapped in intellectual swaddling clothes, of Christians who spoon one another lukewarm Pablum in preference to the meat of strong doctrine. It is a gadget-filled paradise suspended in a hell of insecurity. It is the age of unexamined concepts, limp

62

images, and limber lips. It moves easily from unsupportable hypotheses to foregone conclusions.

—*Foy Valentine*

◇　◇　◇

The sophisticated cruelty of the games people play does not nurture the spirit. Brittle and cynical postures betray many an empty heart.

◇　◇　◇

The worst enemy western civilization faces is not Communism. . . . The worst enemy . . . is within that civilization itself. Our $64 euphemism for it is "secularism." A blunter word is godlessness.

—*Editorial, April, 1949, "Life" Magazine*

◇　◇　◇

Secularism is not a skid-row menace. It is a country-club, Park Avenue menace.

◇　◇　◇

In this blundering world there is a deep homesickness for a God around whom people can center their lives. What men are seeking is not a reasonable theology, but a satisfying God.

—*Joseph R. Sizoo*

◇　◇　◇

We can't deal with moral decline without going to the source—man's sinful heart.

—*Leighton Ford*

◇　◇　◇

What we thought was a fine college ruined our daughter. She took a course in religion which destroyed her faith in the Bible, a course in philosophy which destroyed her faith in God, a course in psychology which destroyed her faith in her parents, a course in biology which destroyed her faith in divine creation, and a course in political science which destroyed her faith in the American way of life.

◇　◇　◇

Man has an innate tendency to worship the creator of what he sees. Much of what modern man sees is man-made. Our paths are asphalt, our canyons concrete and steel, our guidance system electronic, and even our stars are neon! Biblical writers, surrounded by the creations of God, saw God as very much present in His world. They walked the paths of earth between canyons of stone and dirt, not in leisure, but of necessity; they looked at the heavens as much for direction as for speculation.

◇　◇　◇

The division and strife between nations is the divine curse upon human arrogance and pride.

◇　◇　◇

Signs of desperation reveal a day of decline.

◇　◇　◇

In this comfort-conscious, leisure-oriented age we are prone to overlook the importance of self-discipline.

◇　◇　◇

We have descended from the level of being soft about evil to being sentimental about what is downright vile and filthy.

◇　◇　◇

We are captives of the complexities of contemporary life.

◇　◇　◇

In times like these we need less "tele" and more "vision."

◇　◇　◇

Today's choices: super rush, hot rush, and just plain rush.

◇　◇　◇

The prospects never looked brighter, and the problems never looked tougher. Anyone who isn't stirred by both of those statements is too tired to be of much use to us in the days ahead.

　　　　—John W. Gardner in "No Easy Victory"

◇　◇　◇

64

The following is a declaration of a well-known politician: "The budget should be balanced, the treasury should be refilled, the public debt should be reduced, the arrogance of officialdom should be tempered and controlled, assistance to foreign lands should be curtailed lest we become bankrupt. The mob should be forced to work and not depend on government for subsistence."

The politician was Cicero and he was apparently attempting to keep Rome from falling.

◇   ◇   ◇

The healing of social ills comes not from environmental improvement. Man must be changed inwardly. A Chinese proverb says it well: You cannot make a good omelet out of rotten eggs.

◇   ◇   ◇

The challenge to every parent, every church member is for an experience in which God is real, evident, recognizable. Carl Jung, eminent psychiatrist, when asked to diagnose the major spiritual illness of our contemporary society replied, "The central neurosis of our age is emptiness." Viktor Frankl, Viennese psychiatrist, when asked the same question, replied, "Meaninglessness."

◇   ◇   ◇

When man exalts himself, he is thrown into confusion. The channels of communication are destroyed. People became suspicious and frightened of one another.

◇   ◇   ◇

"Now soul and body thrill with joy over the living God" is one translation of Psalm 84:2. This is the thrill our guilt-ridden, nervous, uneasy age needs; a steady confidence in the living God, the relief and freedom of Christian love and forgiveness, the assurance of grace and fellowship in the Christian community. When this experience is ours, not only will we thrill with joy; we will thrill others.

CONTENTION

The church needs workers, not a wrecking crew.

◇ ◇ ◇

Any church can meet opposition from without better than dissension from within.

◇ ◇ ◇

The shallow teapot does the most spouting, and boils dry most quickly.

—*Chinese maxim*

◇ ◇ ◇

The worst wheel of the cart makes the most noise.

—*Benjamin Franklin*

◇ ◇ ◇

If you're hard to get along with, better have your "cranky" case drained.

◇ ◇ ◇

Throwing stones only makes more rocks in the road ahead.

◇ ◇ ◇

No preacher is a prophet just because he disagrees with others.

◇ ◇ ◇

It takes two to make a quarrel, but only one to end it.

◇ ◇ ◇

If you are living a Spirit-filled life, you can't live a contentious life.

CONVERSATION

Cheap conversation betrays a shallow mind.

◇ ◇ ◇

He that converses not, knows nothing.

◇ ◇ ◇

66

The sweetest music isn't in oratorios, but in kind words.

—Ralph Waldo Emerson

◇ ◇ ◇

A gracious word is an easy obligation and pays big dividends.

◇ ◇ ◇

A word fitly spoken in season—how good it is!

CONVERSION

To be ready when Jesus comes means you must be ready before He comes.

◇ ◇ ◇

Very few sinners have ever been converted by the self-righteous.

◇ ◇ ◇

No one has ever become a Christian by accident. There has always had to be a time when he has said, "I will arise and go to my Father."

◇ ◇ ◇

So I come back to where I began, to that other King, one Jesus; to the Christian notion that man's efforts to make himself personally and collectively happy in earthly terms are doomed to failure. He must indeed, as Christ said, be born again, to a new man, or he is nothing. So at least I have concluded, having failed to find in past experience, present dilemmas, and future expectations any alternative proposition. As far as I am concerned, it is Christ or nothing.

—Malcolm Muggeridge

◇ ◇ ◇

The coming of Christ into one's life even now means change: "Old things are passed away; and, behold, all things are become new." New creatures indeed. We are born anew. Born from above. A new nature; a new affection; a new purpose in life; a new reverence for God; a new concern for others; a new discipline of self; a new power to withstand temptation and to resist the lure of the world, the flesh, and the devil; a new hope of eternal life.

◇ ◇ ◇

The moralist and religionist groom the outside and take pride in their appearance, in their reputation, in their image. But they are untouched inwardly; there is no transformation, no death of self and rebirth into a new creature. The "good life" isn't enough. We need a resurrected life.

◇ ◇ ◇

The new birth started you as a child of God; then you must learn, mature, develop, grow.

◇ ◇ ◇

Turning over a new leaf means reform. Turning to a new life means reborn.

◇ ◇ ◇

How does one become a Christian? By repenting of his sins, by confession and restitution, and by turning from his evil life and ways, by obedience to the known will of God, and by the appropriation by faith of the merits of the death of Christ. When all this takes place, one obtains the new birth, which makes him a Christian.

◇ ◇ ◇

We get through to Christ only by a plunge of faith and readiness to take God at His word. Accept Christ, start following Him as you understand Him now! Come to Him as you are. Learn of Him, one lesson at a time, one day at a time. Put Him to the test. But begin where you are.

◇ ◇ ◇

A Christian is a new creature; he has a new heart; lives in a new world; under a new government; serves a new

Master; obeys new laws; is actuated by new motives; influenced by new love; animated with new joys; possesses new delights; and is called by a new name. Yea, all things become new.

◇　◇　◇

Conversion is an instantaneous, climactic, revolutionary event; transition from a life of darkness into one of light; transformation into a new creature.

◇　◇　◇

The Christian idea of conversion isn't basically a certain kind of emotional experience. It means turning around from the slavery of sin to the service of God.

—Leighton Ford

◇　◇　◇

A young woman lived under adverse conditions at home. Frustrated, bitter, unhappy, despairing, no hope for the future. Her discontent was apparent in voice, appearance, manner. However, she found Christ, was born again, and became a transformed person. A friend met her and noticed the smiling face, serene expression, and asked how things were. She replied, "Just the same, but I am different."

◇　◇　◇

Religion is the first thing and the last thing, and until a man has found God and been found by God, he begins at no beginning, he works to no end. He may have his friendships, his partial loyalties, his scraps of honor. But all these things fall into place and life falls into place only with God. Only with God. God, who fights through men against blind force and night and nonexistence; who is the end, who is the meaning.

—H. G. Wells in "Mr. Britling Sees It Through"

◇　◇　◇

Some results of a new life which starts with a born-again experience are:

  —a new fellowship with God
  —a new fellowship with the people of God
  —severance from the sinful past
  —new facing of the present
  —a new outlook toward the future

◇　◇　◇

We try to change circumstances, improve situations. But it is man's nature that needs changing. Our difficulties are within. Patchwork jobs never last. Old things must pass away; all things must become new!

◇　◇　◇

Belief or Christian faith, conversion, is not accepting certain doctrines, or a creed, or what a denomination teaches. It is accepting Christ as Saviour. When we do that we are justified, regenerated, made new, born again, spiritually resurrected from being dead in sin, and are made alive unto God.

COOPERATION

Cooperation is a word that consists of 11 letters—but it can be spelled with 2: WE.

COST OF LIVING

It isn't unlucky these days to have a $2.00 bill. It comes in handy to buy a dollar's worth of most anything.

COURAGE

Channing Pollock told the story of a friend living near Estes National Park in Colorado. He invited Pollock to visit him. He wrote, "We'll take long walks along moun-

70

tain paths and see God's handiwork in its beauty and grandeur." Pollock added, "The bravest thing of all was that my friend could neither walk nor see."

◇　◇　◇

Faith is reason grown courageous.

◇　◇　◇

To dare is great; to bear is greater.

◇　◇　◇

Strange as it may seem, it calls for a great deal of courage really to believe in God.

◇　◇　◇

Courage is fear that has said its prayers.

◇　◇　◇

The test of courage comes when we are in the minority.

COURTESY

Sometimes good manners consist in letting somebody tell you what you already know.

◇　◇　◇

Manners are stronger than laws.

◇　◇　◇

When in doubt, write courteously.

◇　◇　◇

A man is known by the courtesy he shows to lesser folk.

◇　◇　◇

Nothing costs so little as Christian courtesy.

◇　◇　◇

It is not discourteous to refuse to do wrong.

◇　◇　◇

Courtesy costs so little and gets so much.

CRITICISM

Lord, help me to be more critical of myself than others.

◇   ◇   ◇

No man is safe from criticism if he is getting things done.

◇   ◇   ◇

In looking for somebody to criticize, don't turn your head away when passing a mirror.

◇   ◇   ◇

A person who talks about his inferiors doesn't have any.

◇   ◇   ◇

> *The reason that I criticize*
> *And find each person such a pain*
> *Is that to ferret out the good*
> *Would be much harder on the brain.*
>
> *—"Washington Post"*

◇   ◇   ◇

Many people need to throw away their hammers and buy horns.

◇   ◇   ◇

If we are mud slingers we never have our own hands quite clean.

◇   ◇   ◇

People never criticize a corpse.

◇   ◇   ◇

It is easy to ask, "Why doesn't somebody do something?" and then excuse ourselves for not being that somebody.

◇   ◇   ◇

Criticism comes easier than craftsmanship.

◇   ◇   ◇

Children have more need of models than critics.

◇   ◇   ◇

72

How gentle Jesus was with the weak, and how strict He was with those who were guilty of being critical of spirit!

—*Roy Smith*

◇   ◇   ◇

If you have to criticize someone, sandwich it between slices of praise and commendation.

◇   ◇   ◇

You can be sure of one thing: if people criticize you they are interested in you. Not to attract criticism is to live uninterestingly.

◇   ◇   ◇

No man is really educated until he has learned how to use criticism to advantage.

◇   ◇   ◇

The human race is divided into two classes—those who go ahead and do so willingly, and those who sit still and inquire, "Why wasn't it done the other way?"

—*Oliver Wendell Holmes*

◇   ◇   ◇

It is always easy to underestimate the other person's difficulties.

◇   ◇   ◇

Everyone should keep a cemetery in which to bury the faults of his friends.

—*Henry Ward Beecher*

◇   ◇   ◇

Even our critics might have something to say that it would be well for us to hear.

◇   ◇   ◇

Just and fair criticism is all right; but those who give it should keep a generous portion of it for themselves, lest they give the other fellow their own dose.

THE CROSS

A common expression among early American Negroes was: "I have a glory." Jesus said, "I seek not mine own glory"; David said, "In God is my salvation and my glory" (Psalm 62:7); Paul said, "I glory [I take pleasure, satisfaction] in tribulations." What is your glory? It should be, "In the cross of Christ I glory, towering o'er the wrecks of time."

◇ ◇ ◇

The Cross not only brought Christ's life to an end; it ends also the first life, the old life, of every one of His true followers. It destroys the old pattern, the Adam pattern, in the believer's life.

◇ ◇ ◇

The Cross is the evidence of God's redeeming love. It is the fulfillment of God's promise when men fell. It is the realization of all the visions and prophecies throughout the Old Testament. What is its message? That no man need go limping, floundering, in the old way of sin and weakness for another single day. That there is no sin to which we must surrender. That there is no habit which cannot be shattered. That there is no victory that we cannot win through Jesus Christ.

◇ ◇ ◇

Taking up the cross and following Christ is optional. You must decide between two things; you can't have both; there is no third. You can consume your life for your own gratification and profit, satisfy present cravings and tastes. Or you may put aside present enjoyment and interests and devote your life to God and mankind.

◇ ◇ ◇

The challenge of the Cross is not for exceptional courage and occasional heroism, but for a life which in its commonest hours, its regular routine, shall be surrendered and sacrificial.

◇ ◇ ◇

At the foot of the Cross, I seek forgiveness. In the shadow of the Cross, I dedicate myself to serve. In the glory of the Cross, I shall rise to live eternally.

◇　◇　◇

The bedrock of our Christian faith is the unmerited, fathomless marvel of the love of God exhibited on the cross of Calvary, a love we never can and never shall merit.

—*Oswald Chambers*

◇　◇　◇

An advertisement read, "Lovely quality jewelry discreetly decorated with the cross." This is a reminder that the lives of all too many deserve to be described as "discreetly decorated with the cross," because they do not really bear the imprint of the strange Man of the Cross. For these people, the Cross is not the basic structure of life, but merely a prudent ornament. When life is not arranged according to the plan of the Cross, the Cross can be no more than a decoration without reference to the Cross's real meaning.

◇　◇　◇

The Cross is a place of challenge:
- —a challenge to inflexible purpose, to a girded mind.
- —a challenge to love; not merely "in word . . . but in deed and in truth."
- —a challenge to give; to follow Jesus' example.
- —a challenge to go; across the table, the street, the city, the ocean.
- —a challenge to pray; to join Christ in intercession.
- —a challenge to holy living, for "ye are not your own."
- —a challenge to expectancy, for "unto them that look for him shall he appear."

—*J. W. Melick*

◇　◇　◇

The preaching of the Cross is an invitation to the unconverted. To the converted it is a challenge! We need to spend more time at the Cross. It is an excellent place for meditation and edification. To live in the atmosphere of the Cross will put a spiritual health into one's being— a certain fire into the soul. It is here that one may get his directions in life, and gain the right perspective. The Cross is a place of challenge.

—*J. W. Melick*

◇　◇　◇

The cross is an eternal principle, not an incident in history. Ignore it and your life will be worth little in the end. Accept it, follow it, and you will live gloriously, die triumphantly, and reign with Him eternally.

◇　◇　◇

Before the cross of Jesus we are not old or young, educated or ignorant, cultured or uncouth, dull or brilliant; we are just people—human beings lost and ruined deep inside, where incidental differences do not matter, where indeed they are not even known. That about us which yields itself to social differentiation is not that for which Christ died. He died for lost humanity, and anyone can receive the benefits of His atonement, but only as a lost being.

—*"Alliance Witness"*

◇　◇　◇

The center of salvation is the cross of Jesus, and the reason it is so easy to obtain salvation is because it cost God so much.

—*Oswald Chambers*

◇　◇　◇

The badge of Christianity is not a cushion, but a cross.

◇　◇　◇

A shallow faith seems to think that any unpleasantness is the cross Christians must bear. But it is far more than that. A cross is what one bears because of his faith in

76

Christ—misunderstanding, persecution, false accusation, misjudged motives, ridicule, ostracism.

◇　◇　◇

Real involvement means giving of self; it is all tied up in a gospel which culminated in a Cross. Any kind of deep involvement means some kind of cross. Is it a fear of the cross that is making our churches more pagan than Christian? There is no detour to take us around the Cross if we are to find life. Except a grain of corn falls into the earth and there expends itself in an outburst of new life, it is finished. Life begins at the Cross, for it is more than a symbol; it is a reality in the life of each one who gets involved, and the more involved he becomes, the more evident is the cross.

—Dodge, in "The Pagan Church"

◇　◇　◇

For 6 hours, for 2,000 years, it goes on—the traffic along the road beside the Cross, where men and women pass and linger and look or hurry by; and every man's life is changed by the look he gives the stricken Figure on it.

◇　◇　◇

The cross is wrought in gold and hung from the neck of lighthearted beauty; it stands out in bold relief on churches that are filled with easygoing people. The cross has been taken out of Jesus' hands and smothered with flowers; it has become what He would have hated, a source of graceful ideas and agreeable emotion. When Jesus presented the cross to His disciples, He was certainly not thinking of a sentiment that can disturb no man's life nor redeem any man's soul, but of the unsightly beams which must be set up in the midst of man's pleasures and the jagged nails that must pierce his soul.

◇　◇　◇

In order to center our attention and affection upon Christ and the Cross, the world and self must become dead

77

things. As long as the world is attractive to our souls we shall center our glorying in it. As long as self is not crucified we shall glory in our personal attainments, methods, and character. The person who must find his entertainment in the world will not glory in the Cross. The person who must find personal security in himself through realized ambitions in worldly positions, or even in church positions, is not glorying in the Cross.

—William J. Krutza

◇　◇　◇

The Cross must always be an enigma, a stupidity, and anathema to the wisdom of this world. It belongs to the deeps known only to the Spirit and to those enlightened and instructed of Him. The depths of Christ are unsearchable.

—Samuel Chadwick

◇　◇　◇

What is this cross of which the Master is speaking? It is not a mere emblem to be worn in the lapel of the coat, but it is an agency of death, of self-crucifixion, of self-abnegation. It is not one sharp pain and then all is over. It is a life of daily self-surrender and humiliation. It is not a daily crucifixion of the old nature, but a daily crucifixion of the human nature. It is a give-up attitude. It is a surrender, a submission.

—Oliver G. Wilson

DEATH

"The time of my departure is at hand" (2 Tim. 4:6). The actual noun is *analusis,* and how revealingly it describes the death of a Christian! It is a seaman's word—unloosing a ship from its moorings. It is a plowman's word—unloosing a weary team of animals after a hard day's work. It is a traveler's word—striking a tent and continuing the march.

It is a philosopher's word—implying the solution of a problem, the unraveling of a mystery.

◇   ◇   ◇

The measure of a man is best taken after he dies.

◇   ◇   ◇

When the clock strikes for me I shall go, not one minute early, and not one minute late. Until then, there is nothing to fear. I know that the promises of God are true, for they have been fulfilled in my life time and time again. The measure of a life, after all, is not its duration, but its donation. How much will you be missed?

—*Peter Marshall*

◇   ◇   ◇

How much time have YOU left? Now is the day of salvation!

◇   ◇   ◇

If the devil can get you to lying, he will get you when you're dying.

◇   ◇   ◇

Some people who expect salvation at the eleventh hour die at ten-thirty.

◇   ◇   ◇

No one ever repented of being a Christian on his deathbed.

◇   ◇   ◇

When the sun goes below the horizon, it is not set; the heavens glow for a full hour after its departure. And when a great and good man dies, the sky of this world is luminous long after he is out of sight. Such a man cannot die out of this world. When he goes he leaves behind much of himself. Being dead, he speaks.

—*Henry Ward Beecher*

◇   ◇   ◇

No one flies over the Valley of the Shadow. You walk its rocky paths, step by step.

—*Catherine Marshall*

◇　◇　◇

Death is only an old door
Set in a garden wall;
On gentle hinges it gives,
At dusk when the thrushes call.
Nothing can trouble the heart,
Nothing can hurt at all.
Death is only a quiet door
Open, in an old wall.

—*Anonymous*

◇　◇　◇

He has left behind him, in the memory of his life, a striking exemplification of the power, the dignity, and the majesty of the Christian religion.

◇　◇　◇

When all is done, say not my day is o'er,
And that through night I see a dimmer shore;
Say rather that my morn has just begun—
I greet the dawn and not a setting sun,
When all is done.

—*Paul Lawrence Dunbar*

◇　◇　◇

Death is not extinguishing the light; it is putting out the candle because the dawn has come.

◇　◇　◇

To live in hearts that are left behind is not to die.

DEBTS

Don't nose around too much. You are your brother's keeper, but not his bookkeeper.

◇　◇　◇

80

The man who won't pay his debts should remember that God made man out of dust, and dust settles.

◇　◇　◇

Some men are known for their deeds, others for their mortgages.

DECISION

Life is rooted in choices and is constantly carried forward by choices.

—D. T. Niles

◇　◇　◇

Be careful how and what you choose. Minor choices in daily routine of living become guiding principles that later govern our thinking and actions.

◇　◇　◇

Personal interest plays some part in our decisions—usually about 99 percent.

◇　◇　◇

You will never have a favorable wind if you do not know to which port you are sailing.

DEFEAT

The devil doesn't want us to discard our religious faith; he wants us to dilute it.

◇　◇　◇

We accommodate ourselves to inadequacy, to low levels of performance in spiritual things, when:
    —our ideals aren't lofty enough
    —our standards are not high enough
    —our self-discipline is not severe enough
    —our desire for Christlikeness is not intense enough
    —our commitment is not complete enough

◇　◇　◇

In *Screwtape Letters,* C. S. Lewis creates a senior devil, Screwtape, who writes to his nephew, Wormwood, a junior devil who has been given the responsibility of causing the spiritual defeat of a new Christian. In one of his letters Screwtape writes to Wormwood, "Indeed, the safest road to Hell is the gradual one—the gentle slope, soft underfoot, without sudden turnings, without milestone, without signposts."

◇　◇　◇

One way to always lose is to be a quitter.

◇　◇　◇

Spiritual malnutrition results from being satisfied with so little spiritual food.

◇　◇　◇

If you are going to the Lord every few days with the same defeats, there is something lacking in your life.

◇　◇　◇

When you feel like coasting, you are either losing momentum or going downhill.

◇　◇　◇

The decision of the moment is the outcome of all the past.

DEPRESSION

If you must be blue, be bright blue!

◇　◇　◇

The Sermon on the Mount will lift you out of the valley.

◇　◇　◇

When you're down in the mouth, remember Jonah; he came out all right.

DESTINY

Choice, not chance, determines human destiny.

◇　◇　◇

The way you face decides your destiny.

THE DEVIL
Resist the devil; take him by surprise. Release, relief, and reckless delight will be yours if you dare to stand your ground and plead the blood of Christ!

◇ ◇ ◇

The devil is never too busy to rock the cradle of a sleeping saint.

DISAGREEMENT
Making a lot of noise doesn't constitute a sound argument.

◇ ◇ ◇

The man who is interested in blowing his own horn is seldom interested in harmony.

◇ ◇ ◇

You can't see eye to eye with a man you look down on.

◇ ◇ ◇

Even a watch that is stopped is right twice every 24 hours.

◇ ◇ ◇

It is difficult for some people to believe you are a Christian if you do not agree with them.

◇ ◇ ◇

It's all right to disagree. Just don't be disagreeable.

◇ ◇ ◇

Let us define our terms before we start the argument.

DISAPPOINTMENT
Life's disappointments are veiled Love's appointments.

◇ ◇ ◇

When handed a lemon, don't get upset; just add sugar and make lemonade.

DISCIPLESHIP

It costs to be a Christian. For a true faith finds its expression in living. The Christian walk crosses the ideas and ideals of a sinful world, and so Christian living involves taking up a cross. A crossless life is not truly Christian. It is not an easy thing to be a disciple of Christ.

◇　◇　◇

Quite necessary to Christian discipleship is consecration. But equally necessary is application.

◇　◇　◇

Salvation is free because it was paid for by Another. But discipleship is a very different thing. Discipleship is costly.

DISCIPLINE

Beware of the danger of relaxation spiritually.

—Oswald Chambers

◇　◇　◇

A young mother inquired of General Robert E. Lee how best she could bring up her young son for God. "Teach him to deny himself!" was the reply.

◇　◇　◇

An element in abiding, in keeping spiritually alive, in keeping deadwood cleared and conserving our energies for fruit bearing, is discipline.

◇　◇　◇

One of the great failures of our generation has been to underestimate the importance of discipline. Influenced by a superficial psychology, we have abhorred restraint, indulged our natural impulses, and crucified inhibitions. We forget too easily that no worthwhile or significant life or work is possible without discipline.

◇　◇　◇

People and nations, like trees, are destroyed from the

84

inside. Even the lack of vigorous spiritual exercise invites moral weakness. There is no such thing as spiritual triumph in the absence of moral effort.

—*Arnold E. Airhart*

◇ ◇ ◇

The discipline of affliction is but for the moment. If borne in faith, it yields fruit as a tender plant, the peaceable fruit of righteousness that pleases God and lifts humanity nearer to heaven.

—*Frank Alfred Mathes*

◇ ◇ ◇

A disciplined Christian is cheerful when it is difficult to be cheerful, patient when it is difficult to be patient; he pushes on when he would like to stand still; he keeps silent when he perhaps has a right to be belligerent and disagreeable. The reason is so simple: he has learned self-discipline.

◇ ◇ ◇

Another name for self-discipline: directed stubbornness.

◇ ◇ ◇

Discipline: what we need most and want least.

◇ ◇ ◇

The natural man craves comfort, ease, self-indulgence. The Apostle Paul said, "I keep under my body, and bring it into subjection."

◇ ◇ ◇

It would be a far better world if people would do themselves what they tell their children to do.

◇ ◇ ◇

A pat on the back will work wonders with a spoiled child— if given with proper force in the right place.

DISHONESTY

A shady business dealing never yields a sunny life.

DISPOSITION

The leopard cannot change his spots, and even if he did, the transformation would not change his disposition.

DOUBT

As long as you are a doubter you can't be a shouter.

DRESS

Of all the things you wear, the most important costs nothing—your expression.

DUTY

The best way to get rid of duties is to discharge them.

◇　◇　◇

The consciousness of duty well done gives us music at midnight.

◇　◇　◇

It always seems easy to see the other man's duty.

◇　◇　◇

One's need constitutes another's opportunity and prescribes his duty.

EASTER

The three most sublime words: He Is Risen.

◇　◇　◇

The Resurrection showed men the reality and beauty of God's eternal power and they knew that darkness and sin and evil, tyranny and torture and death, could never again have the last word—

> Whatever clouds may veil the sky,
> Never is night again.

No, never! There broke from that garden on Easter morning the first rays of everlasting joy, and nothing, nothing, NOTHING can take from us the certainty that in the end that light will be in our hearts, that joy our possession forever.

—*Leslie Weatherhead*

◊　◊　◊

Does the truth of Easter thrill you? Is it a way of life, as it was with early Christians? Does it fill you with wonder, adoration, joy, hope, assurance?

◊　◊　◊

He is risen! Go and tell!

EDUCATION

It's what you learn after you know it all that counts.

◊　◊　◊

To make a college education a success one must be willing to learn something after leaving college.

◊　◊　◊

Education will broaden the narrow mind, but it takes religion to cure the big head.

◊　◊　◊

Henry Sloane Coffin in his inaugural presidential address at Union Theological Seminary in New York City in 1926 laid down four ideals for a seminary: scholarship and solid learning; churchmanship in which there is "one church, hospitable and homelike to all disciples of Jesus Christ"; worshipfulness; an enthusiasm in which there is the "kindling in all those who study here a passion for the worldwide kingdom of Christ."

◊　◊　◊

He is best educated who is most useful.

◊　◊　◊

Christianity is the mother of modern education.

◊　◊　◊

Education without God is like a ship without a compass.

◇   ◇   ◇

Does education pay? Does it pay to sharpen tools before beginning work?

EMERGENCIES

If you would be used in a large way, make good in the small emergencies.

◇   ◇   ◇

If you don't meet up with emergencies, they catch up with you.

EMPATHY

Of three major figures in modern psychiatry, Freud says that man wants most of all to be loved; Jung, that he wants most of all to feel secure; Adler, that he wants to feel significant.

◇   ◇   ◇

In a world of spiritual darkness because of sin; in a world of physical need—hunger, suffering, neglect—give us concern for the needy, compassion for the suffering, understanding for the troubled.

◇   ◇   ◇

Your pain is in my heart also.

ENEMIES

A man without enemies is a nobody.

ENTHUSIASM

Enthusiasm in politics and recreation, fervour in reform and business, intensity in work and friendship, are among

88

the most coveted qualities of modern life. In religion they are bad form. Enthusiasts in piety are suspect. Christians full of zeal are merely tolerated where they are not despised. They are regarded as intellectually inferior.

—*Samuel Chadwick*

◇   ◇   ◇

Put your heart into your work and the quality of your work will put your heart into you.

◇   ◇   ◇

The proper amount of emotional coloring is an asset to any personality; too much of it is a liability.

◇   ◇   ◇

If you show people you're a live wire, they won't step on you.

◇   ◇   ◇

Enthusiasm is a good engine, but it needs intelligence for a driver.

◇   ◇   ◇

We like people who can roll a ball uphill. Most anyone can roll one downhill.

◇   ◇   ◇

When the church ceases reaching out for the unsaved, it is time for an awakening. No cause succeeds without passion, enthusiasm, aggressiveness. When so-called Christians languish in creature-comfort, eyes blind and ears deaf to the plight of the unchurched and unsaved, the drift from God is already under way.

◇   ◇   ◇

A crudely emotional approach to religion is preferable to religious formalism which is purely aesthetic and orderly but lacking in dynamic power. One of our serious troubles in the church today is that it has become legitimate to be emotional about anything but religion. The need is for something that will summon one's whole enthusiasm. The moment the church becomes completely programized and depersonalized, it becomes a monument to God's memory and not an instrument of His loving power.

—*John A. Mackay*

◇   ◇   ◇

Enthusiasm has been defined as magnificent madness.

◇   ◇   ◇

We need enthusiasm in our religious life; we need it in our secular pursuits; we need it in our human relationships, in our affection for our loved ones and our friends, in our casual contacts with those we meet only occasionally. Enthusiasm is contagious, it is therapeutic, it is effective; it often accomplishes what otherwise would be impossible.

◇   ◇   ◇

Most ministers will agree that rarely do they speak to an enthusiastic congregation. As Dr. Henry Sloane Coffin said, "A minister's task is mainly to organize the zeal of his people." He continued to lament that "heartiness has fallen out of fashion, or rather our times lack the conditions which create it. The gospel has to fetch it from God and set hearts ablaze."

◇   ◇   ◇

Enthusiasm is passé in our modern, sophisticated, blasé, thrill-surfeited society. To be enthusiastic one must be stirred; to be stirred one must be observant of situations that need remedying, of causes that need supporting, of issues that need antagonizing, of truths that need proclaiming. And who wants to be bothered? Who wants to become involved in another's distress, or danger, or dilemma? But it is still true as Emerson said, "Nothing great was ever accomplished without enthusiasm."

90

EVANGELISM

As long as the heart has passions, as long as life has woes, as long as man's life is haunted by the thought of the infinite, as long as sin and death inflict their fearful wounds, the words of Christ will live. His gospel is an everlasting gospel.

—*Clarence E. Macartney*

◇ ◇ ◇

You know that nothing communicates fire except fire.

◇ ◇ ◇

Christian penetration may be altogether valid, but it must not be uncouth.

—*Robert A. Williams*

◇ ◇ ◇

Go appears 1,200 times in the New Testament. *Teach,* 216 times. *Preach,* 175 times.

◇ ◇ ◇

I am not afraid of the Communists; I am not afraid of the Catholics. I am afraid of some of the Protestants who have neither fire nor vision; of men who begin to see why any idea of outreach might be hard, or unprecedented, or premature, or not properly surveyed, or too informal, or too big. The put-on-the-brakes type, the go-slow type can ruin God's program.

O ye of little faith, keep your foot off the brake! Who ever heard of God holding us back?

—*Frank Laubach*

◇ ◇ ◇

Christianity is no longer indispensable when it must resort to gimmicks and trivia to win its world.

—*Robert A. Williams*

◇ ◇ ◇

There are too many churches with flawless credentials of

orthodox theology whose outreach is almost nil. They are "sound" but they are sound asleep.

◇   ◇   ◇

Oswald J. Smith's oft-repeated statement has become a Christian classic: "The supreme task of the Church is the evangelization of the world," to which he bluntly added, "Not one pastor in 100 believes it! Not one church in 1,000 believes it! Not one Christian in 10,000 believes it!"

◇   ◇   ◇

Without evangelism a church is in danger of becoming a chubby, clubby, complacent collection of nice folks—a sort of closed shop for the edification of the saints.

◇   ◇   ◇

It is impossible to overestimate the concern of God for a lost world. Do we share that concern?

◇   ◇   ◇

Evangelism is the normal, day-after-day attitude of all Christians. Those who know Christ must share their experiences of Him with others.

◇   ◇   ◇

Too many churches lack the concern of the New Testament fellowship to penetrate the world around with the Good News.

◇   ◇   ◇

Make evangelism your vocation. Say with the Apostle Paul, "For to me to live is Christ."

◇   ◇   ◇

Evangelism in the New Testament Church was characterized by a sense of urgency: "Now is the day of salvation." What has happened to this sense of immediacy?

◇   ◇   ◇

We need evangelism today—in the pulpit, in the pew. We need personal and public evangelism. Reproduction is the normal function of a church which is alive.

◇　◇　◇

Whenever the vital power of the Christian gospel exists in some life there will be the spread of the gospel to other lives.

◇　◇　◇

The great need of the Church today is not some plan, but the certainty, the confidence, the courage to take the offensive and to be possessed by a passion to tell the Good News in the radiance of a compelling love for men.

◇　◇　◇

To receive the love of God into one's heart is to receive the compelling urge to win others.

◇　◇　◇

Evangelism is the plan of God for spreading the gospel. It is the anguished lament of Jesus as He weeps over Jerusalem. It is the cry of Paul, "I could wish that myself were accursed from Christ for my brethren." It is the prayer of John Knox, "Give me Scotland or I die!" It is George Whitefield, worn and ill, getting out of bed and coming back to speak to the Crown until the candles go out—and dying the next morning. It is Harmon Schmelzenbach begging, with tears, to be sent back to Africa to die!

◇　◇　◇

It sometimes happens that a well-kept church lawn is good evangelism.

◇　◇　◇

The "evangel" is the Good News, and "evangelism" is telling it!

EXAMPLE

People look at me six days a week to see what I mean on the seventh.

◊　◊　◊

Christianity is the good man's text; his life, the illustration.

◊　◊　◊

A Christian is a person who makes it easier for others to believe in God.

◊　◊　◊

The gospel according to you! Does it save from sin and worldly compromise? Or is it a gospel of expedience? Does it keep you calm when things go wrong? Serene under pressure? Kind in the face of antagonism? Does it give you victory in adversity, illness, and reverses?

◊　◊　◊

A good example is a powerful sermon.

◊　◊　◊

Few essential doctrines are in need of being defended. What they need is to be demonstrated.

◊　◊　◊

Your life is a sermon to others: what kind of preacher are you?

◊　◊　◊

Nothing is so infectious as example.

EXCUSES

You never will make a success peddling excuses, for you will find that the people you contact are well supplied.

◊　◊　◊

Of all human inventions the most worthless is an excuse.

◊　◊　◊

94

An excuse is so many times just a falsehood substituted for a reason.

◇　◇　◇

No man can excuse himself on the basis that he has faith God will work.

◇　◇　◇

It is usually very easy to accept our own excuses.

◇　◇　◇

It is always easy to find excuses when we can't find reasons.

EXERCISE

Jumping to conclusions is all the exercise some folk take.

EXPERIENCE

We make much of the crises in Christian experience, and well we should. Being born of the Spirit and filled with the Spirit are not process experiences; living the Christian life is. The Psalmist was concerned "that I may daily perform my vows." Someone has said that the secret of walking with God is to make sure that the miracle of the new birth is renewed daily. Not, of course, the actual occurrence, but the wonder of it, the effect of it, must not subside or wear off.

—*M. A. Lunn*

◇　◇　◇

Unless we are careful, second-generation Christianity may become an impersonal inheritance instead of a living experience.

◇　◇　◇

Some people learn from their experiences; others never recover from them.

◇　◇　◇

Past experience should be a guidepost, not a hitching post.

◇ ◇ ◇

Experience is a wonderful thing. It enables you to recognize a mistake when you make it again.

◇ ◇ ◇

Experience is what you get while you are looking for something else.

◇ ◇ ◇

Experience joined with common sense,
To mortals is a providence.

FAILURE

To fail while doing your best is still a gain.

◇ ◇ ◇

No failure need be final.

◇ ◇ ◇

No man has failed just because he has not lived up to his mother's expectations.

◇ ◇ ◇

Climb up on your stumbling blocks instead of falling over them.

◇ ◇ ◇

Failure is the lot of.him who neglects to use what he has.

◇ ◇ ◇

The difference between success and failure is that one wills to do and the other only wishes it could do.

◇ ◇ ◇

No professional success can ever quite atone for one's personal failure.

◇ ◇ ◇

The man who halted on third failed to make a home run.

◇ ◇ ◇

Dishonest success is a low form of failure.

◇ ◇ ◇

Failure is not the worst thing in the world. Not to try is.

◇ ◇ ◇

The upright man can never be a downright failure.

◇ ◇ ◇

Not failure, but low aim, is crime.

—*James Russell Lowell*

◇ ◇ ◇

Many a man gets left because he didn't do right.

◇ ◇ ◇

A halfhearted attempt is a wholehearted failure.

FAITH

Faith is not mere belief. It is belief plus what you do with that belief. Belief becomes faith only at the point of action.

◇ ◇ ◇

Are you putting your faith to work or is it merely something to make you feel comfortable?

◇ ◇ ◇

Faith is not belief without proof but trust without reservation.

◇ ◇ ◇

Faith is God's decisive answer to the chaos of the world. Faith is hope when all expectancy has died; courage when you are terrified; light when you walk in darkness; forgiveness when you have blundered badly; friendship when you are feeling lonely and forsaken; and at last, a welcome home from the Lord of life eternal when your day is turned to sunset and the evening star is in the sky.

—*James Stewart*

◇ ◇ ◇

The faith of the Early Church Christians: faith as clear as the sunlight, as enduring as a granite mountain! What a vital thing is faith! All round us are theological millinery, fads, fancies, cults, and innovations such as religions of prosperity. The New Testament Christians were as unshakable as Gibraltar. They suffered privation, imprisonment, torture—things from which the human recoils. Paul said, "I glory [take pleasure, satisfaction, pride] in tribulations."

◇   ◇   ◇

This life of faith is not a life of mounting up with wings, but a life of walking and not fainting.

—*Oswald Chambers*

◇   ◇   ◇

Faith is the entire process through which, because of what we believe, we appropriate to our needy hearts all that the grace of God has made possible for us.

◇   ◇   ◇

Jesus said that if your faith had the right quality you didn't need much of it. Just a tiny amount would enable you to do the impossible. Not a day passes but that things impossible in the natural realm are brought to pass because of faith.

◇   ◇   ◇

Faith is man's response to God's grace.

◇   ◇   ◇

Keep the faith amid life's weariness and defeat and apparent failure. Keep it though your most cherished ambitions fall in wreck about you. Keep it in the day of prosperity and in the night of adversity. Keep the faith when hopes are high and when discouragement lays its leaden weight on the soul. Keep the faith through moods and melancholy. Keep the faith though poverty should press to your lips her hard crust.

◇   ◇   ◇

Keep the faith and all losses will not amount to much. If you lose the faith, all other gains will not amount to much.

◇   ◇   ◇

There is such a faith as meets disappointments, disaster, disillusionments with a firm: "Sirs, I believe God." Such a faith adds up to a religion of reality.

◇   ◇   ◇

Faded faith will flame anew when from the heart there is offered and answered the prayer, "But take the dimness of my soul away."

◇   ◇   ◇

Faith is the response of your total self: will, intellect, emotions—the whole works—to Jesus Christ.

◇   ◇   ◇

Our faith is the entire scope of our belief in God and the resultant attitudes and actions.

◇   ◇   ◇

Faith is positive, certain, sure. The moment doubt enters and faith wavers, there is no longer faith.

◇   ◇   ◇

We limit God by not implementing what we believe; by not letting His power transform us; by not making His presence real; by following a course of human wisdom when we affirm God's omnipotence but don't let His power enable us to do exploits for Him.

◇   ◇   ◇

> Let me no more my comfort draw
> From my frail hold on Thee;
> In this alone rejoice with awe—
> Thy mighty grasp of me.

◇   ◇   ◇

A faith that is strained, that a seeker has to be "argued

99

and pushed into," is likely to be premature and hence a
spurious faith.

—*Richard S. Taylor*

◇　◇　◇

To be faithful is to be fruitful.

◇　◇　◇

Many a man's faith is about as deep as that of the boy
who said, "We say our prayers at night. We are not afraid
in the daytime."

◇　◇　◇

Christian faith is assuring, insuring, enduring.

◇　◇　◇

The great enemy of the life of faith in God is not sin, but
the good which is not good enough. The good is always the
enemy of the best.

—*Oswald Chambers*

◇　◇　◇

Faith is more of a way of walking than of talking.

◇　◇　◇

Faith isn't revealed until it is tested.

◇　◇　◇

Faith never demands that we deny facts.

◇　◇　◇

No man has faith just because he submits to the inevitable.

◇　◇　◇

The heart of a man's faith is what he thinks about God.

◇　◇　◇

He is rich who is rich in faith.

◇　◇　◇

Faith is the soul riding at anchor.

◇　◇　◇

Faith is believing what God says without asking any questions.

◇   ◇   ◇

Faith can never overdraw its account.

◇   ◇   ◇

Faith, like a roll of film, is best developed in the dark.

◇   ◇   ◇

Faith is not believing that God can; it is knowing that He will.

◇   ◇   ◇

While there is faith, there is hope.

◇   ◇   ◇

A little faith can go a long way.

◇   ◇   ◇

Believe you can do a thing, and it's half done before you start.

◇   ◇   ◇

Too many people want faith the size of a mountain before they attempt to move a mustard seed.

◇   ◇   ◇

Faith means human weakness laying hold of divine power.

◇   ◇   ◇

Trusting God for the impossible is Christian faith.

◇   ◇   ◇

Faith is something much more significant than an orthodox theological opinion.

◇   ◇   ◇

Faith is never faith until it gets into action.

◇   ◇   ◇

Every Christian must exercise his own faith.

◇   ◇   ◇

Faith brings us to God; Hope anchors us to God; Love makes us like God.

◇   ◇   ◇

It is the darkness which makes faith a reality.

◇ ◇ ◇

The beginning of real faith is the end of anxiety.

◇ ◇ ◇

I do not see my way, but I know that He sees His way, and that I see Him.

◇ ◇ ◇

Real faith never goes home with an empty basket.

FAITH, DEFENSE OF
Living one's faith is the best method of defending it.

◇ ◇ ◇

The trouble with some people is that they cannot defend their faith without fighting someone equally as faithful.

FAITHFULNESS, LOYALTY
There is no greater merit than faithfulness.

◇ ◇ ◇

Loyalty is the holiest good in the human heart.

FAMILY ALTAR
The family altar would alter many a family.

◇ ◇ ◇

Daily prayers are the best remedy for daily cares.

◇ ◇ ◇

The family altar will keep out of the home the undesirable intrusions of modern life.

◇ ◇ ◇

Henry M. Grady visited Washington, D.C., and when he went back to Atlanta, Ga., he wrote an editorial about the Capitol at Washington, describing it beautifully and calling it the home of this great nation, the center of American life. A few months later, however, he revisited his old home in rural Georgia. This time, back in Atlanta, he wrote another editorial in which he said that he had made a tremendous blunder when he wrote the first one. He said that the center of this country is not in the Capitol of the United States—rather it is in the cottages and in the old farmhouses and in every home in this land in which there is a family altar. The Christian home is the center of American life from which all the rest of the country moves and radiates!

◇   ◇   ◇

Seldom is there a broken home when the family altar is kept up.

FAME

The more important the man, the more he owes of personal service to his church and community.

◇   ◇   ◇

The man who wakes up to find himself famous hasn't been asleep.

FAULTFINDING

No man ever built himself up by tearing another man down.

◇   ◇   ◇

It's smart to pick your friends, but not to pieces.

◇   ◇   ◇

If you blow out another man's candle it will not light your own.

◇   ◇   ◇

An inch of progress is worth more than a yard of faultfinding.

◇   ◇   ◇

It is always easier to find fault than it is to produce results.

◇ ◇ ◇

Before you count your neighbor's faults, stop, count 10—
of your own.

◇ ◇ ◇

It is usually much easier to find faults than it is to find
remedies.

◇ ◇ ◇

No man gets very high by tearing other people down.

◇ ◇ ◇

The only fellow we know who makes anything running
people down is the elevator operator.

◇ ◇ ◇

You have to be little to belittle.

◇ ◇ ◇

Correct your own faults when you see the errors of others.

◇ ◇ ◇

Don't forget—the woodpecker is the only one that ever gets
anywhere by knocking, and he always ends up in a hole.

◇ ◇ ◇

If you want to set the world right, start with yourself.

◇ ◇ ◇

Praise loudly; blame softly.

◇ ◇ ◇

Opportunity never knocks at the door of a knocker.

◇ ◇ ◇

When using a hammer, build something.

◇ ◇ ◇

Faultfinding is one talent that should be buried and the
place forgotten.

◇ ◇ ◇

The easiest thing to find is fault; the hardest thing to keep
is silence.

FAULTS

The greatest of all faults is to imagine you have none.

FEAR

Faith dissipates fear.

◇   ◇   ◇

If you fear, cast all your cares on God; that anchor holds.

—*Alfred Lord Tennyson*

◇   ◇   ◇

I do not fear the road ahead when I remember the road behind.

—*Hugh Redwood*

◇   ◇   ◇

Fearless minds climb soonest unto crowns.

◇   ◇   ◇

Fear has defeated more men than actual trouble has.

◇   ◇   ◇

Fears can age you more than years.

◇   ◇   ◇

Keep your eyes on God and your fears will vanish.

—*Gaston Fuoye*

◇   ◇   ◇

The answer to fear is faith.

◇   ◇   ◇

Wear lightly the garment of life—there are no fears, only those we create.

◇   ◇   ◇

The Bible teaches us to fear God, and nothing else.

FLATTERY

Flattery does not hurt unless you inhale it.

◇   ◇   ◇

Enjoy the fragrance of flattery, but do not swallow it.

FORGETTING

When God pardons, He consigns the offense to everlasting forgetfulness.

◇   ◇   ◇

Remember, it pays to forget those things which are behind.

FORTUNE TELLING

The fortune-teller was addressing one of her clients: "You will be poor and unhappy until you are 40."

"And after that?"

"You'll get used to it."

FREEDOM

Most people in the United States believe strongly in free enterprise. But sometimes we forget that freedom and duty always go hand in hand, and that if the free do not accept social responsibility, they will not remain free.

—*John Foster Dulles*

FRIENDSHIP

Be slow in choosing a friend; be slower in changing one.

◇   ◇   ◇

It takes a lot of forgiving to be a friend.

◇   ◇   ◇

A man is known by the company he does not keep.

◇   ◇   ◇

No man lacks friends who has the gift of appreciation.

◇   ◇   ◇

One kind of enemy is a friend who does not oppose you when you are wrong.

◇ ◇ ◇

Confidence is the backbone of friendship.

◇ ◇ ◇

The best mirror is an old friend.

◇ ◇ ◇

Give your friends the benefit of that doubt.

◇ ◇ ◇

Our chief want in life is somebody who shall make us do what we can. This is the service of a friend.

—*Ralph Waldo Emerson*

◇ ◇ ◇

True friends are the finest of all God's gifts;
They are precious and very rare.
They come with a love that laughs and lifts
When the burdens are hard to bear.
They are true when the sun is ablaze in the skies,
When life is bright and fair.
When sorrow or pain has dimmed your eyes,
There's compassion and tenderness there.

—*Lorie C. Gooding*

◇ ◇ ◇

Sometimes, on the road of life,
We meet the sort of friend
Who's set apart from others—
That rare and perfect blend
Of all the things a friend should be.
In fact, a friend like you—
How glad I am our pathways crossed!
I'm hoping you are, too!

◇ ◇ ◇

Fair-weather friends are plentiful and pleasant, but blessed is the friend who shares our rainy days.

◊ ◊ ◊

Dr. Smiley Blanton suggests that we learn the value of the tender touch. This eminent physician talks about the healing power of simply touching someone you love. An invisible virtue seems to leave one body and find itself to the other by touch. Dr. Blanton suggests walking with your arm around your wife or holding hands around the dinner table when you say grace.

◊ ◊ ◊

My best friend is the one who brings out the best in me.

—*Henry Ford*

◊ ◊ ◊

What is friendship? It is many things—

It is feeling completely natural with another, shedding all pretense and sham, just being yourself.

It is sharing with another both big and little things, joy and sorrow, laughter and tears.

It is counting on another to understand your moods, to put up with your failings, to be there when you need him most with a word of encouragement, a smile, a look.

How do I know what friendship is? I know because you are my friend, and you are all these things.

◊ ◊ ◊

A blessed thing it is for any man or woman to have a friend: one human soul whom we can trust utterly; who knows the best and the worst of us, and who loves us, in spite of all our faults; who will speak the honest truth to us, while the world flatters us to our face, and laughs at us behind our back; who will give us counsel and reproof in the day of prosperity and self-conceit; but who will cheer us in the day of difficulty and sorrow, when the world leaves us alone to fight our own battle as we can.

—*Charles Kingsley*

◊ ◊ ◊

Ay, there are some good things in life
That fall not away with the rest.
And, of all best things upon earth,
I hold that a faithful friend is the best.

◊ ◊ ◊

A boy in school was far gone with homesickness, walking with a coat collar turned up, across a wet campus on a dreary, stormy day. He was lonely and discouraged. He heard a friendly voice say, "Walk with me, lad," and a professor extended his umbrella. Instantly clouds vanished and the boy was happy and hopeful once more, glad to be in college. Through succeeding years the professor's umbrella has seemed to be over him. Now he says, "To walk with him through college years was to walk with him forever."

◊ ◊ ◊

Give me the love of friends, and I
Shall not complain of cloudy sky,
Or of little dreams that fade and die.
Give me the clasp of one firm hand,
The lips that say, "I understand,"
And I shall walk on holy land.
For fame and fortune burdens bring,
And winter takes the rose of spring;
But friendship is a Godlike thing.

—*Anonymous*

◊ ◊ ◊

Mrs. Robert Browning inquired of Charles Kingsley, "What is the secret of your life? Tell me, that I may make mine beautiful, too." He replied, "I had a friend."

◊ ◊ ◊

The man with no friends has already abandoned himself to the fate of his own self-destruction.

—*Karl Menninger*

◇　◇　◇

I love you not only for what you are, but for what I am when I am with you. I love you not only for what you have made of yourself, but for what you are making of me. I love you because you have done more than any creed could have done to make me good, and more than any fate could have done to make me happy. You have done it without a touch, without a word, without a sign. You have done it by being yourself. Perhaps that is what being a friend means, after all.

—*Anonymous*

◇　◇　◇

Oh, the comfort, the inexpressible comfort of feeling safe with a person; having neither to weigh thoughts nor measure words, but to pour them all out, just as they are, chaff and grain together, knowing that a faithful hand will take and sift them, keep what is worth keeping, and then, with the breath of kindness, blow the rest away.

—*George Eliot*

FUTURE LIFE
The house which you see now is only a prologue to what it is to be.

◇　◇　◇

Eternal life is a gift of God, apprehensible here and now. We live in it when we are in conscious union with Christ. Eternity begins, not at death, but at conversion, when Christ takes control of me.

—*Brazier Green*

◇　◇　◇

110

Over the door in the Cathedral of Milan is to be found the inscription "Only the Eternal is important!"

◇ ◇ ◇

Where are you going—eventually?

◇ ◇ ◇

Where you go hereafter depends on what you go after here.

GENERATION

There is one eternally lasting, therefore vitally important, good one generation can pass on to the next. Give the young people a saving knowledge, a personal relationship with Jesus. This we can do; this we must do!

◇ ◇ ◇

Every generation needs to rethink, restate, and creatively apply its theological heritage to its own situation. In this way the heritage stays vital, and relevant.

—*Mildred Bangs Wynkoop*

◇ ◇ ◇

The generation that cannot learn from the past will never understand the future.

◇ ◇ ◇

Regeneration today means a better generation tomorrow.

GENIUS

To think straight in a crooked world is real genius.

GIVING

He who gives promptly gives twice as much.

◇ ◇ ◇

Some church folks are like sponges. They absorb all and give nothing unless tightly squeezed.

◇ ◇ ◇

111

Give, for the years are passing.
Give freely; all too soon
The noonday follows sunrise,
The sunset follows noon.
Place love lamps in the window;
Bless others while you may.
Today the door stands open;
Tomorrow—who can say?

◇   ◇   ◇

He is dead whose hand is not open wide
To help the need of a human brother;
He doubles the length of his lifelong ride
Who gives his fortunate place to another;
And a thousand million lives are his
Who carries the world in his sympathies.
To give is to live!

◇   ◇   ◇

If taking an offering in church hurts the spirit of the meeting, it is not God's Spirit, for He does not advocate a miserly attitude toward the church or His work.

◇   ◇   ◇

Those who give most are least concerned about returns.

◇   ◇   ◇

Take time to give.

◇   ◇   ◇

A generous man is always sorry he cannot give more.

◇   ◇   ◇

Give not from the top of your purse but from the bottom of your heart.

◇   ◇   ◇

Most of us enjoy giving when it gratifies our vanity, but that is hardly to be called Christian charity.

◇   ◇   ◇

112

Frugality is good if liberality be joined with it.

◇ ◇ ◇

One does not need to have a large income to be stingy.

◇ ◇ ◇

In this world it is not what we take up and keep that makes us rich, but what we give up to the other fellow.

—*Henry Ward Beecher*

◇ ◇ ◇

God never fails to make a note of our generosity, even if the world does not thank us.

◇ ◇ ◇

Two marks of a Christian are giving and forgiving.

◇ ◇ ◇

God loves a cheerful giver—until he brags about it.

◇ ◇ ◇

Every unconsecrated dollar is excess baggage.

◇ ◇ ◇

Giving is participating in the work of God.

◇ ◇ ◇

A kind deed often does more good than a large gift.

◇ ◇ ◇

You may give without loving but you cannot love without giving.

◇ ◇ ◇

We make a living by what we get, but we make a life by what we give.

◇ ◇ ◇

What you keep to yourself you lose; what you give away you keep forever.

GOALS

Aim at heaven and you will get earth thrown in. Aim at earth and you will get neither.

—*C. S. Lewis*

◇ ◇ ◇

Don't drift aimlessly from day to day; choose a worthwhile goal and steadfastly advance toward it.

◇ ◇ ◇

Set fresh goals for yourself.

◇ ◇ ◇

The young fellow who doesn't know where he is going won't find much when he gets there.

—*C. A. McConnell*

◇ ◇ ◇

The man without an aim never makes a hit.

◇ ◇ ◇

Some people have the right aim in life but they never pull the trigger.

◇ ◇ ◇

The reason so many people miss their mark or goal is because they just shoot, without taking aim at anything.

◇ ◇ ◇

It is better to aim for a high goal and miss it than to aim low and leap clear over it.

◇ ◇ ◇

Those who aim at nothing always hit it.

◇ ◇ ◇

Plateaus are made for resting—and planning which peak to aim for next.

GOD

We think little about God if we think much about ourselves.

◇ ◇ ◇

How big? God is big enough to satisfy all the longings of the soul!

◇ ◇ ◇

No one ever finds God who does not feel himself in need of God.

◇ ◇ ◇

History is the hand of God writing in terms of human life.

◇ ◇ ◇

Good: God is *for* us. Better: God is *with* us. Best: God is *in* us.

◇ ◇ ◇

God has worked some surprising results with some imperfect people.

◇ ◇ ◇

God can do nothing for us unless we let Him.

◇ ◇ ◇

God has two dwellings: one in heaven, and the other in meek and thankful hearts.

◇ ◇ ◇

One with God is a majority.

◇ ◇ ◇

One of the unique aspects of the Christian religion is that God communicates with His people. In no other religion does its deity offer this relationship.

◇ ◇ ◇

Teach me so to live as being always in Thy presence.

◇ ◇ ◇

Indeed, I tremble for my country when I reflect that God is just.

—*Thomas Jefferson*

◇ ◇ ◇

Liken your Christian life to a wheel of which you are the rim. If you could move to the center where God is found, you would discover peace; for at the hub, the center, there is peace. There you will find stillness and the power to create your own world within a world.

◇ ◇ ◇

There is no night so dark, but Thou canst light the way out and guide me safely through. No problem so complicated but Thou canst solve and help me find the right solution. No tangle so snarled but Thou canst undo the kinks. No circumstance so hopeless but Thou canst help me surmount it. No present so dismal but Thy presence can make it glorious. No future so uncertain but Thou dost send a ray of hope. No adversity so distressing but Thou canst bring peace and calm and trust. No grief so overwhelming but Thou wilt comfort and sustain!

◇ ◇ ◇

O Lord, my God, help me now to find in Thee what I cannot find out of Thee: rest and peace and joy, which abide with me only as I abide in Thee. Lift up my soul above the weary round of harassing thoughts to awareness of Thee and to the atmosphere of Thy eternal presence, that there I may draw strength from Thy eternal life continually.

◇ ◇ ◇

There is but one answer to the prevailing mood of the world and the Church. It is to come face-to-face with a relevant, involved, present God.

◇ ◇ ◇

Whenever men forsake the God who made them, man-made gods begin to appear. When will we learn that there is no substitute for the living God?

◇ ◇ ◇

A God who is not personal, with whom we cannot communicate, is merely a nebulous idea, a theory, a philosophy. The Christian's God is a reality, ever present, available, a God of adequate resources all of which are at our disposal. This God indwells, empowers, guides, comforts, upholds.

◇   ◇   ◇

In all His dispensations, God is at work for our good. In prosperity He tries our gratitude; in mediocrity, our contentment; in misfortune, our submission; in darkness, our faith; under temptation, our steadfastness; and at all times, our obedience and trust in Him. God governs the world and we have only to do our duty wisely and leave the issue to Him.

—*John Jay, of the U.S. Supreme Court*

◇   ◇   ◇

God's laws are inviolable, sacred, not to be broken.
God's standards are changeless.
God's judgments are inevitable, unavoidable, certain.
God's love is limitless, steadfast.
God's mercy endureth forever.
God's promises are sure, trustworthy.

GOD'S CARE

All places are safe; all losses are profitable; all things work together for good to them that love God.

◇   ◇   ◇

If a righteous God rules our universe, then no evil is ever permanent, no matter how powerful.

◇   ◇   ◇

God cares for both the spiritual and the physical well-being of the individual.

117

GOD FIRST

The self-life has been conquered when we can say with the Apostle Paul, "I glory in tribulations." To glory means to "reach the highest degree of pleasure, satisfaction, and pride." That's the pinnacle of commitment. That's putting God first literally.

◇　◇　◇

Be serious with God and leave the rest gaily alone.

—Oswald Chambers

◇　◇　◇

Anything that becomes our master is dangerous. Any affection, interest, or hobby, or avocation that usurps the time and attention which should be devoted to the things of God is sinful.

◇　◇　◇

How tragic for anyone to live in a self-centered world of indulgence in fleshly gratification, of limiting his aspirations to fleeting pleasures of earth while the joys of eternal bliss are ignored!

◇　◇　◇

Anything you put before God; anything in your affections, your choices, which you give priority over the claims of God, is your treasure . . . and there will your heart be!

◇　◇　◇

Better to run into heaven barefooted and bareheaded than to miss it because of anything in this world.

GOD'S GRACE

We take grace and its blessings for granted, as if we had them coming. Easy-come, easy-go religion, emotionally dependent on the ties of custom and association; a thinly disguised hankering after the world; an absence of a burst-

118

ing sense of joyous gratitude; a scarcity of that loving, humble mindfulness of the miracle of grace which has saved us!

◇　◇　◇

We are not meant to be superhuman paragons of godliness, but by the common stuff of ordinary living to exhibit the marvel of the grace of God.

◇　◇　◇

Don't let the blinding clouds of worldly interests obscure from our spiritual eyes the beauties of God's grace.

◇　◇　◇

Never-diminishing springs of grace flowing from the heart of God—ever flowing from the heart of God, ever flowing from generation to generation; "streams of mercy, never ceasing," amid the striving and sinning of man—sufficient to supply our most tragic needs and to satisfy our deepest yearning! Amazing grace!

◇　◇　◇

Given
Received
Accepted
Confirmed
Embraced

◇　◇　◇

Life really begins for us when we are healed in the very depths of our natures by the love, the grace of God.

◇　◇　◇

There is no such thing as cheap grace!

—*Dietrich Bonhoeffer*

◇　◇　◇

In the New Testament this sentence appears 10 times: "The grace of our Lord Jesus Christ be with you." *Grace*

119

appears 92 times; *grace of God* appears 24 times; *grace of our Lord Jesus,* 12 times.

◇ ◇ ◇

Grace is the unmerited favor, the forgiveness, the wisdom, the power, the love of God, freely bestowed upon the undeserving sinner.

◇ ◇ ◇

Grace is energy; grace is love-energy; grace is redeeming love-energy ministering to the unlovely and endowing the unlovely with its own loveliness.

—John Henry Jowett

◇ ◇ ◇

Grace is God's enabling power freely given, that we may triumph continually in this hostile world.

◇ ◇ ◇

We can face any situation fortified by the faith and courage God's grace provides.

GOD, KNOWING HIM

God, when He comes, comes only on the feet of doves, and we must be still.

—Helmut Thielecke

◇ ◇ ◇

Begin to know Him now, and finish never.

—Oswald Chambers

◇ ◇ ◇

The difference between knowing God in the full-orbed glow of His presence and living in the half-light of an unsatisfactory Christian experience is that important factor of spiritual receptivity—or call it spiritual response.

◇ ◇ ◇

Oh! that I might repose on Thee. Oh! that Thou wouldst enter into my heart, and inebriate it, that I may forget my ills, and embrace Thee, my sole good.

—St. Augustine

◇   ◇   ◇

Narrow is the mansion of my soul; enlarge Thou it, that Thou mayest enter in.

—St. Augustine

◇   ◇   ◇

The way of Christ is the way to the heart of God.

◇   ◇   ◇

Man has only one way to God, and that is through Jesus Christ.

◇   ◇   ◇

O Thou who art the Light of the minds that know Thee, the Life of the souls that love Thee, and the Strength of the wills that serve Thee; help us so to know Thee that we may truly love Thee; so to love Thee that we may fully serve Thee, whom to serve is perfect freedom.

—St. Augustine

◇   ◇   ◇

No one knows God at His best who holds Him off at arm's length.

GOD, SEEKING HIM

The blind man was desperate; he called the more loudly. He would not be hushed. He created a disturbance. He joined his need with his belief and with his quest. He put everything he had into his effort.

◇   ◇   ◇

God speaks to those who are still enough to listen.

GOLDEN RULE
The golden rule will not work by itself. You will have to work it.

GOODNESS
Goodness is the only investment that never fails.

GOSSIP
If you begin to throw dirt, you lose ground.

◇　◇　◇

Some people are like blotters. They soak it all in but get it all backwards.

◇　◇　◇

Plant a little gossip and you will reap a harvest of regrets.

◇　◇　◇

When parrots repeat what they hear, unlike people, they do not add to it.

◇　◇　◇

When tempted to gossip, breathe through your nose.

◇　◇　◇

Some people never go into action at a dinner party until the body of an innocent absentee is put on the carving block.

◇　◇　◇

Even gossip will disappear if there is no market for it.

◇　◇　◇

Gossip is a vulture who delights in feasting on the heartaches and miseries of others.

◇　◇　◇

Many a gossiper has opened his mouth and gotten his foot into it.

◇　◇　◇

122

Bad for the heart: running upstairs and down people.

◇   ◇   ◇

If you take good heed to what in yourself you are inwardly, you will not care what men may say about you.

—*Thomas a Kempis*

◇   ◇   ◇

A little gossip goes a long way.

◇   ◇   ◇

More people are run down by gossip than by automobiles.

GRATITUDE

To be thankless is to be joyless.

◇   ◇   ◇

A grateful heart is always a prayerful heart.

◇   ◇   ◇

Get out of Grumble Lane and live on Thanksgiving Street.

◇   ◇   ◇

Be thankful for many things you haven't got.

◇   ◇   ◇

The best prayer is one of thanksgiving.

GREATNESS

It is not the square miles but the square people who make a nation great.

◇   ◇   ◇

The caliber of a man is indicated by the size of the things that offend him.

◇   ◇   ◇

A man is as big as the things which annoy him.

◇   ◇   ◇

The greatest truths are the simplest and so are the greatest men.

◇   ◇   ◇

He that is good is ever great.

◇　◇　◇

If you cannot do great things, you can do small things in a great way.

◇　◇　◇

If you want to be great, don't try to be.

◇　◇　◇

Great is the man who does not lose his child's heart.

◇　◇　◇

The greatest men are those whose defeats have not defeated them.

◇　◇　◇

The great in the Bible lived close to God.

◇　◇　◇

Your greatness is measured by the size of the wrong you can forgive.

◇　◇　◇

The greater man, the greater courtesy.

◇　◇　◇

We all make footprints on the sands of time, but some leave the print of a great soul, others just the heel.

◇　◇　◇

The greatest man is the one who always does what he knows is right.

◇　◇　◇

A great man is one who can have power and not abuse it.

◇　◇　◇

God, the greatest Giver; His Son, the greatest Gift; Eternal life, the greatest possession.

◇　◇　◇

Competition is between those trying to be great, not between those who are.

GRUDGES

A grudge grows bigger and heavier when carried.

GUIDANCE

When we fear that we may not know the meaning of God's will, we had better turn to himself for clear guidance and safekeeping.

—G. Campbell Morgan

◇ ◇ ◇

The trainer of Seeing Eye dogs told his blind companion as he crossed the street with her and her guide dog, "Walk closer to him. He cannot guide you if you hold him at arm's length." So speaks God to you.

◇ ◇ ◇

If we let God guide, He will provide.

◇ ◇ ◇

Instead of divine guidance being a spiritual luxury for rare souls, it is a minimum necessity for every Christian. "As many as are led by the Spirit of God, they are the sons of God" (Rom. 8:14).

◇ ◇ ◇

We cannot expect guidance from God until His will, not our own, becomes supreme.

◇ ◇ ◇

One reason for so little divine guidance is that it strikes at the center, the citadel of personality and demands surrender of self-sufficiency.

◇ ◇ ◇

Most people are circumstance-directed, instead of being Christ-directed.

◇ ◇ ◇

Guidance must mean receptivity. We must feel, "Thy will

be done," with enthusiasm; not, "Thy will be endured."

◇   ◇   ◇

Reasons for divine guidance:
1. God knows our nature as no one else does.
2. God knows the future as no one else does.
3. God has a purpose for us such as no one else does.

◇   ◇   ◇

He who, from zone to zone,
  Guides through the boundless sky thy certain flight,
In the long way that I must tread alone,
  Will lead my steps aright.
                              —*William Cullen Bryant*

◇   ◇   ◇

If our hearts are right, if we are fully committed, God guides our common sense, our outlook, our disposition, inclination, tendency. It isn't necessary to say constantly, "Now, Lord, what is Thy will?"

◇   ◇   ◇

When in doubt concerning God's will, do nothing. God doesn't expect us to do anything under a cloud. He may not show you the whole course, but He will make the first step clear. Do not take it until He does.

◇   ◇   ◇

How can we expect God to speak in emergencies when we have refused to listen to Him for so long?

◇   ◇   ◇

We cannot get light in a crisis unless we are willing to get light in the continuous.

◇   ◇   ◇

Beware of shortcuts in guidance.

◇   ◇   ◇

God's great clarifier in guidance is waiting; like clearing a glass of muddy water.

126

HABITS

Established routine, good habits, are God's way of saving us between the times of uplift and mountaintop experiences and the dull, drab, even dismal days of ordinary, lackluster living. We learn to live through days of drudgery by faith and the grace of God.

◇ ◇ ◇

The chains of habit are too weak to be felt until they are too strong to be broken.

◇ ◇ ◇

Bad habits are like a comfortable bed: easy to get into, hard to get out of.

◇ ◇ ◇

Mark well your habits! They will either make or mar you.

◇ ◇ ◇

One way to break a bad habit is to drop it.

◇ ◇ ◇

A man's character is the sum of his habits.

HAPPINESS

Happiness is the distinctive mark of a Christian.

◇ ◇ ◇

There is only one way to be happy and that is to make somebody else so.

◇ ◇ ◇

Happiness is a habit; cultivate it with a smile.

◇ ◇ ◇

Happiness is losing yourself in something you believe to be worthwhile.

◇ ◇ ◇

Happiness, like pure gold, is rarely found in huge nuggets, but is scattered in precious, glittering particles through the common rock of daily living. It is only when we gather these shining particles together that we realize how rich we are in joy.

◇　◇　◇

God's will and our highest personal good are that we be holy and useful. Nor can these two be separated. "The holy man will be the useful man." And the curious outcome of it is that he is apt to be the happy man, also.

—*W. T. Purkiser*

◇　◇　◇

To be the happiest you must forget self.

◇　◇　◇

Dr. Albert Schweitzer was asked, "Have you found happiness in Africa?" He replied, "I have found service, and that is happiness enough for anyone."

◇　◇　◇

The first step toward real happiness is a step toward God.

◇　◇　◇

Many persons have a wrong idea about what constitutes true happiness. It is not attained through self-gratification, but through fidelity to a worthy purpose.

—*Helen Keller*

◇　◇　◇

Happiness is being so absorbed in some task that one forgets himself.

◇　◇　◇

The four-year-old son came in from the backyard in a general state of disarray.

"You're a mess!" his mother scolded.

"Yes," agreed the youngster, "but I'm happy."

◇　◇　◇

Happiness is essentially and inevitably a by-product that comes invariably by indirection. "Overtaken by joy."

◇　◇　◇

Happiness is bound up with helpfulness.

◇　◇　◇

The Declaration of Independence guarantees your right to the pursuit of happiness, but you have to catch up with it yourself.

◇　◇　◇

Certainly our religion should be a source of goodness. But it should be the source of gladness as well. Holiness should not only minister to piety; it ought to contribute to happiness also.

—"Herald of Holiness"

◇　◇　◇

Happiness multiplies as we divide with others.

◇　◇　◇

We cannot have happiness until we forget to seek for it.

◇　◇　◇

Happiness is victory over sorrow.

◇　◇　◇

Letting a little sunshine in is good, but don't forget to let a little sunshine out.

◇　◇　◇

Happiness is the halfway station between too much and too little.

◇　◇　◇

It is difficult to define happiness. But we know when we find it, and we know when we lose it. We know that most people are looking for it. We know that it isn't anything that anyone can bestow on anyone else. Others may help make it; others often impair it; but it is something that grows inside ourselves.

◇　◇　◇

The only way to keep happiness is to give it to someone else.

◇　◇　◇

It isn't your position, but your disposition, that makes you happy or unhappy.

◇   ◇   ◇

Happiness must be used daily. You cannot preserve it.

◇   ◇   ◇

You have no right to consume happiness without producing it.

◇   ◇   ◇

There is no happiness in things.

◇   ◇   ◇

Real happiness begins where selfishness ends.

◇   ◇   ◇

Those who bring sunshine into the lives of others cannot keep it from themselves.

◇   ◇   ◇

Happiness is the perfume you cannot pour on others without getting a few drops on yourself.

◇   ◇   ◇

Happiness is attained through fidelity of purpose.

◇   ◇   ◇

Blessed are the happiness makers.

◇   ◇   ◇

Unselfishness and happiness are twins.

HARMONY

To have a good time at the expense of an uneasy conscience does not pay. To have an enemy if we can have a friend does not pay. Nor does it pay to sow wild oats if we have to buy our own crop. It does not pay to give God the husks instead of the heart. A life of harmony is attained by obedience to God, unselfish living, and an upright walk through a distracting and sinful world.

◇   ◇   ◇

130

Calm is the soul that is emptied of all self, in a restful harmony.

—*Dag Hammarskjöld*

◇ ◇ ◇

My idea of an agreeable person is one who agrees with me.

—*Samuel Johnson*

◇ ◇ ◇

It is always better to explain matters than to allow a good friend to go on wondering.

◇ ◇ ◇

When you pull on the oars you don't rock the boat.

◇ ◇ ◇

God loves a fighter—in a good cause.

◇ ◇ ◇

God's people may work in complete harmony, but not always in complete understanding.

HATE

What a wonderful world this would be if people hated sin as they do people!

◇ ◇ ◇

I will let no man drag me down so low as to make me hate him.

—*Booker T. Washington*

◇ ◇ ◇

Hate never builds anything. It can only blast.

◇ ◇ ◇

Hate always comes home to roost.

HEART

What's in the heart is more important than what's in the head.

HEAVEN

Heaven is a prepared place for a prepared people.

◇　◇　◇

Alexander Whyte would cry out at the close of a sermon: "What will it be to be there?" Then he would add, "Aye, and what will it be not to be there?"

◇　◇　◇

To get to heaven turn to the right and keep straight ahead.

◇　◇　◇ ˌ

If the way to heaven be narrow, yet it is not long; and if the gate be straight, it opens into endless life.

—Bishop Beveridge

◇　◇　◇

A 98 percent Christian almost makes heaven.

◇　◇　◇

You cannot legislate the human race into heaven.

◇　◇　◇

On earth you can gain only one thing permanently— heaven.

HELP

If you would lift me up, you must be on higher ground.

◇　◇　◇

Do not expect help when you are unwilling to give it.

◇　◇　◇

The only people to get even with are those who have helped you.

◇　◇　◇

The best place to find a helping hand is at the end of your own arm.

◇　◇　◇

You can't do much towards helping a person who will not try to help himself.

◇　◇　◇

The Lord also helps those who help others.

HOLINESS

We need a heart-washing, as well as a heartwarming experience a good many times in the process of living in a dirty world. We cannot learn a few simple, and easily practiced rules of human conduct which are acceptable to some ecclesiastical style-maker, and substitute them for character issuing from a pure heart.

—Charles A. McConnell

◇　◇　◇

If we are going to retain personal contact with the Lord Jesus Christ, it will mean there are some things we must scorn to do or to think, some legitimate things we must scorn to touch.

—Oswald Chambers

◇　◇　◇

Holiness means disciplined living, self-forgetfulness, putting God first, and seeking to be of service to others.

◇　◇　◇

Be pure as snow, but don't drift.

◇　◇　◇

God's standard is holiness. It is written: "Holiness, without which no man shall see the Lord" (Heb. 12:14).

◇　◇　◇

Christian perfection means single-mindedness; altogether yielded; completely given over to God; no inward divisions.

◇　◇　◇

Holiness is a totalitarian response to God.

◇　◇　◇

The holiest of men . . . still need Christ as their King, for God does not give them a stock of holiness. But unless they receive a supply each moment, nothing but unholiness would remain. . . . Even perfect holiness is acceptable to God only through Jesus Christ.

—*John Wesley*

◇　◇　◇

Holiness bears sorrow without murmuring, hopes without fatigue, submits without dictating, follows without hesitating, has its "fruit unto holiness, and the end everlasting life."

◇　◇　◇

Activate the principle of perfect love to your brethren, to the unlovely; unselfish service to others.

◇　◇　◇

Holiness is a crisis in that moment of trust for cleansing from all sin by the blood of Jesus Christ. And it is a process, as there must be a maintained condition of purity by moment-by-moment obedience and trust.

—*Thomas Cook*

◇　◇　◇

Some are trying to be Christians in a mild sort of way, vainly trying to find happiness without holiness. Thus they live their pinched, meagre little lives, and die their little deaths, and are laid in their little graves, without ever experiencing the "abundant life" which is the unceasing concern of the Saviour, who came "that they might have life, and that they might have it more abundantly."

—*Charles W. Koller*

◇　◇　◇

There is a perfection that is definite, decisive, and determinate; and there is a perfection that is progressive, disciplinary, and ethical.

—*Samuel Chadwick*

◇　◇　◇

Holiness means unsullied walking with the feet, unsullied talking with the tongue, unsullied thinking with the mind —every detail of the life under the scrutiny of God.

◇   ◇   ◇

As committed Christians are continually filled with the Spirit, there is outward evidence of the inner miracle.

—Eunice Bryant

HOLY SPIRIT

"They were all filled with the Holy Ghost."
Filled like a stream with banks flooded.
Like tides flowing in from the ocean.
Like the sails of a ship are filled with wind.
Like the aroma of perfume filling a room.
Like a sanctuary is filled with tones of an organ.
Here are movement and attraction; advance and progress; influence and fragrance; expression and worship.

◇   ◇   ◇

The human spirit fails unless the Spirit fills.

◇   ◇   ◇

The Holy Spirit comes as fire to purify, as wind to cleanse, as light to reveal.

◇   ◇   ◇

It is the Spirit that quickens. Everything else fails. The letter may be faultlessly orthodox, the method may be marvelously ingenious, the man may be tremendously earnest, but only the God-made, God-inspired, God-enabled avails. Carnalities kill. The power that quickly transforms, perfects, is the God of the Spirit.

—Samuel Chadwick

◇   ◇   ◇

There is no doubt that the one thing needful for the Church is the blessing of Pentecostal fullness. The flood

135

would sweep away all rubbish, fill all the dykes, and fertilize all the desert.

—*Samuel Chadwick*

◇   ◇   ◇

I do now tremblingly accept the blessed truth: God the Spirit; the Holy Spirit; who is God Almighty, dwells in me. O my Father, reveal within me what it means, lest I sin against Thee by saying it and not living it.

—*Samuel Chadwick*

◇   ◇   ◇

No power on earth or in hell can conquer the Spirit of God in a human spirit. It is an inner inconquerableness.

—*Oswald Chambers*

◇   ◇   ◇

The Spirit seeks partnership with us. His resources are inexhaustible! His power invincible! But! But! But! There are reserves, conditions, interests, barriers that hinder, grieve, and quench the Spirit. He is held up by unbelief and prayerless living, worldly ambition, stupid vanity, and inflated pride.

—*Samuel Chadwick*

◇   ◇   ◇

A great many people are afraid to be filled with the Spirit of God—afraid of being called fanatics. You are not good for anything until the world considers you a fanatic.

◇   ◇   ◇

God forbid that we should resist the Holy Spirit as He seeks to alert, liberate, awaken, renew.

◇   ◇   ◇

If the Spirit of Jesus comes to live in me, then I can live a life that reflects His character and spirit.

136

HOME/FAMILY

I have known parents who would tell the kids, "A little bird told me," and then whale the stuffing out of them for trying to kill the canary.

◇　◇　◇

Make your home more than just a refueling place for the children.

◇　◇　◇

The most essential element in any home is God.

◇　◇　◇

Very few houses are big enough for two spoiled parents.

◇　◇　◇

The hearthstone is still the nation's cornerstone.

◇　◇　◇

A good many houses ought to be remodeled into homes.

◇　◇　◇

TEEN-AGE JOE: Whassa idea of wearing my raincoat?
BROTHER BILL: You wouldn't want me to get your new suit wet, wouldja?

◇　◇　◇

Churchgoing families are happier.

◇　◇　◇

The only trouble with child psychology is that children don't understand it.

◇　◇　◇

The most influential of all educational factors is the conversation in a child's home.

—William Temple

◇　◇　◇

The ornament of a house is the friends who frequent it.

—Ralph Waldo Emerson

◇　◇　◇

Every person needs a citadel where he can be esteemed, a citadel where his selfhood is respected, where he is not lost as a person.

◇   ◇   ◇

The home should be a center of more shared fun, with more give-and-take, more discussions and decisions. Home should be a meeting place of love and faith where family members do much more listening to one another, and communicating with one another, in moments of intimacy and sympathetic concern and fellowship.

◇   ◇   ◇

A graduate student doing research on juvenile delinquency at the University of Wisconsin reported difficulty in collecting data. His project was to telephone a dozen homes at night at about nine o'clock to ask parents if they knew where their children were at that hour. "My first five calls," he lamented, "were answered by children who did not know where their parents were."

◇   ◇   ◇

The vital factor of building a Christian home is atmosphere, and the basic ingredient of this atmosphere is love. Wherever love rules, there is an atmosphere, a climate of congeniality, warmth, of protective sheltering.

◇   ◇   ◇

A number of graduate students at the University of Chicago, when asked where they got their major ideas in morals and religion, replied, "Through the conversation in our family at mealtime."

◇   ◇   ◇

While Woodrow Wilson was president of Princeton, he was called upon to speak to the Alumni Association. After his speech he was asked by one of the fathers present why he did not make more out of their boys. Mr. Wilson is

138

quoted as having replied, "Gentlemen, because they are your boys."

◇ ◇ ◇

Six hundred students at one university were asked to vote on the most beautiful word in the English language. 422 wrote, "Mother." 112 wrote "Home."

◇ ◇ ◇

Family—
> When you're hungry they feed you;
> When you're cold they shelter you;
> When you're bad they forgive you;
> When you're disconsolate, they cheer you.

◇ ◇ ◇

A Japanese girl during college holidays visited in the home of an American classmate. At the end of the visit someone asked her what she thought about the American home. Her reply was that she enjoyed every moment of it. She was received warmly and comfortably cared for. She was puzzled by one thing, though. The family worshipped on Sunday along with other Christian people, but during the week there was no reference to God in the conversation, nor did the family pray together.

◇ ◇ ◇

A Christian family sat in the office of a realtor. The mother was holding the baby. A five-year-old pulled excitedly at his father, who stood reading the sale agreement. Handing the boy a piece of candy, the realtor said, "I just sold your daddy a home." The boy quickly replied, "We didn't need a home. Daddy, Mommy, Baby, and me, we are a home. We only want a house to put it in."

HONESTY
Seek no honor that is not based on honesty.

HOPE

You have to believe the buds will blow—
Believe in the grass in the days of snow.
Ah! this is the reason the bird can sing.
On his darkest day he believes in spring!

◇ ◇ ◇

God, give me hope that through these dark days shall come the light of better days.

HUMILITY

The meekness and humility which the grace of God imparts releases from the tyranny of our ego.

◇ ◇ ◇

Our good is never good enough, our virtue is never virtuous enough, our piety is never pure enough to enable us to be other than humbly prostrate before the God of all.

—Harold Bosley

◇ ◇ ◇

Being humble involves the willingness to be reckoned a failure in everyone's sight but God's.

—Roy M. Pearson in "Here's a Faith for You"

◇ ◇ ◇

Humble pie never bothers one's indigestion.

◇ ◇ ◇

The higher a man is in grace, the lower he will be in his own esteem.

—Charles H. Spurgeon

◇ ◇ ◇

It is not a great thing to be humble when you are brought low, but to be humble when you are praised is a rare and great attainment.

◇ ◇ ◇

Let your light shine without turning the spot on yourself.

◇   ◇   ◇

Humility, a blessed grace, smooths the furrows of care, and gilds the dark paths of life. It will make us kind, tender-hearted, affable, and enable us to do more for God and the gospel than the most fervent zeal without it.

—*Henry Martyn*

◇   ◇   ◇

If the shoe fits, buy it and wear it, even though it does reveal the true dimensions of your feet.

◇   ◇   ◇

God enters life through humble hearts.

◇   ◇   ◇

The yoke of Christ will not fit a stiff neck.

◇   ◇   ◇

The poor in spirit are protected from the tyranny of the opinions and comments of others. They possess the spontaneous, free, unconcerned joy of those who live in God's world, unintimidated, free, with joy, and no false pride.

HUMOR

I'd rather see a portrait of a dog I know than all the allegorical paintings in the world.

—*Samuel Johnson*

◇   ◇   ◇

EMPLOYEE: I must have a raise. Three companies are after me.
BOSS: Who are they?
EMPLOYEE: The light company, the water company, and the phone company.

◇   ◇   ◇

A man is as old as he feels; a woman, as old as she feels—
like admitting.

◇   ◇   ◇

A synonym is a word used in place of one you can't spell.

—*Stokes*

◇   ◇   ◇

Poetic: Lo, the morn!
Realistic: Mow the lawn!

◇   ◇   ◇

Wife, *to absentminded professor*: "Your hat is on the
wrong way, dear."
Professor: "How do you know which way I'm going?"

◇   ◇   ◇

"Talk about dumb waitresses! I asked for extract of beef
and she brought me a glass of milk!"

◇   ◇   ◇

Someone told me that men are now going to the beauty
shop for permanent waves. Well, as for me, I would be
satisfied with permanent hair, without the waves.

◇   ◇   ◇

Gift for the man who has everything: a prehistoric fish
skeleton, antiqued.

HYMNODY

Christianity is a singing faith.

◇   ◇   ◇

Isaiah's vision was inspired by the chanting of 400 Levites.
The return from captivity inspired the writing of the one
hundred thirty-sixth psalm, sung antiphonally, "His
mercy endureth for ever."

◇   ◇   ◇

After the Bible in importance, to any people, is its hymnol-
ogy. If one is forced to choose between the privilege of

preaching what the people are to believe or of teaching them the songs they will sing, he might wisely choose the latter.

◇　◇　◇

Song is the natural speech of the emotions. When the heart is stirred, it sings. Music not only expresses, but intensifies, the feelings.

◇　◇　◇

From the days of the apostles to the last church revival, it is true that when the Spirit of God moves mightily the people burst into song.

◇　◇　◇

The Lollards filled all England with their singing, and the followers of Luther struck terror into the Catholic hierarchy by their carols. The Wesleyans announced by their singing that a new epoch in Christian history had dawned.

◇　◇　◇

There is a Lamech singing in the early dawn of the history of every people, and a Jubal fashioning harps and pipes. The Jewish church seized upon this natural aptitude and made use of it in the Temple service, in every synagogue, and in every Jewish home.

◇　◇　◇

Music is a form of power which may be used for the creation of an atmosphere in which the Christian finds delight.

◇　◇　◇

> Scarce seen, scarce heard, unreckoned,
>   Despised, defamed, unknown,
> Or heard but by our singing,
>   On, children! ever on!
>   —Gerhard Teersteegen

◇　◇　◇

Sing on then, Christians, teachers, children! May there be not a few who hear and learn to love the story of the Cross

143

by singing it. Sing on, fellow traveler, and may there meet you in the "better land" many a redeemed soul washed and made white, to whose mortal ear your voice is familiar and who will give thanks eternally for being led thither by the sanctified influence of your song.

—*P. P. Bliss*

◇　◇　◇

The wise young man in the Book of Job spoke of God, "who giveth songs in the night" (Job 35:10); and the Psalmist said of the Lord that even "in the night his song shall be with me, and my prayer unto the God of my life" (Ps. 42:8).

◇　◇　◇

The soul cannot adore God adequately in "me-centered" songs. There is some place in worship for songs which talk about me, my feelings, and my experience; but when the worshiper wishes to adore his Creator and Redeemer, the hymns must focus upon Him, exalt Him, and thank Him.

—*Paul M. Miller*

◇　◇　◇

Praise and thanksgiving in worship expressed through music help unite worshipers in spite of the things which tend to divide them.

◇　◇　◇

Praise expressed through music helps the worshiper to march triumphantly over his own doubts.

◇　◇　◇

Hymns of praise and adoration can prepare one for a glimpse of God's glory.

◇　◇　◇

Adoration is an essential element of true worship and is frequently best expressed through music.

◇　◇　◇

J. H. Jowett years ago referred to the words of the Christian Apollinaris in Ibsen's *The Emperor Julian* as he

144

looked at the great army of the emperor massed against the soldiers of the Cross: "Verily I say unto you, so long as song rings out above our sorrows, Satan shall never conquer!" Dr. Jowett added, "I too will say that our praise is an invincible armour—we sing our way to the triumph we seek!"

◇　◇　◇

When troubles come, go at them with songs. When griefs arise, sing them down. Lift the voice of praise against cares.

—Henry Ward Beecher

◇　◇　◇

Keep a song in your heart each day;
　It will make the whole world brighter,
And smooth the roughness of the way;
　Every burden will be lighter.

◇　◇　◇

In the hymns of the Church, disappointments, heartaches, a thousand perplexities and annoyances have all been buried deep in the grave of oblivion.

◇　◇　◇

Singing makes every movement rhythmic, every service praise, every act thanksgiving.

◇　◇　◇

Keep a song in your heart despite circumstances. "This too shall pass."

◇　◇　◇

Certainty: "He lives! He lives!"
Purity: "He abides; Christ abides."
Loyalty: "I'll live for Him who died for me."
Confidence: "Where He leads me, I will follow."
Outreach: "Make me a blessing."
Commitment: "I'll go where You want me to go."

◇　◇　◇

Sing when times are dark—you will make them bright; sing when the house of life is lonely—it will become peopled with unseen choristers; go down into the valley of shadow with a song—and you will find yourself singing the new song of Moses and the Lamb when you awake on the other side.

—*F. B. Meyer*

HYPOCRISY

What dishonesty is to a banker and what palsy is to a surgeon, lovelessness is to a Christian.

◇　◇　◇

A religion of mere emotion and sensationalism is the most terrible of all curses that can come upon any people. The absence of reality is sad enough, but the aggravation of pretense is a deadly sin.

—*Samuel Chadwick*

◇　◇　◇

Much of the criticism voiced by young people today is directed toward the phoniness of adults. Adults may be regarded as phonies in that they may say they believe in one thing and behave in ways that deny their beliefs.

—*Edwin L. Becker*

◇　◇　◇

Some men get up in church on Sunday and loudly berate themselves as sinners. Then on Monday they go out and prove it.

IDEALS

Lofty ideals often live in a lowly place.

◇　◇　◇

Some people I have known will fall for most any old thing and stand for nothing.

◇　◇　◇

146

You cannot live big with small ideals.

◇ ◇ ◇

The greatest curse is to be satisfied with low ideals.

◇ ◇ ◇

Reaching high keeps a man on his toes.

IDLENESS

"The whole armour of God" is awkward equipment for an easy chair.

◇ ◇ ◇

The idle Christian is the raw material of which backsliders are made.

◇ ◇ ◇

What a fellow does when he has nothing to do is many times the acid test that he fails in.

◇ ◇ ◇

Caution: Easy Street often becomes a blind alley.

◇ ◇ ◇

Dream castles are all right until you try to move into them.

IDLE TALK

It is the shallow brook that babbles.

◇ ◇ ◇

An ounce of action is worth a pound of chatter.

◇ ◇ ◇

Talking too much usually follows thinking too little.

◇ ◇ ◇

A word once spoken can never be recalled.

◇ ◇ ◇

The trouble with most people who have nothing to say is that they are not happy until they say it.

◇ ◇ ◇

You may be able to read some folks like a book, but you can't shut them up nearly as easily.

◇ ◇ ◇

You wish some guys were on TV—so you could turn them off.

◇ ◇ ◇

If some people had to eat their words they would die of indigestion.

◇ ◇ ◇

Blessed is the man who, having nothing to say, abstains from wordy evidence of the fact.

◇ ◇ ◇

Are you known by your objectives or your adjectives?

◇ ◇ ◇

It takes a strong man to hold his own tongue.

◇ ◇ ◇

Great talkers; little doers.

—*Benjamin Franklin*

IGNORANCE

Ignorance is free but the upkeep is tremendous.

◇ ◇ ◇

Slang is a device for making ignorance audible.

◇ ◇ ◇

The recipe for perpetual ignorance: Be satisfied with your opinions and content with your knowledge.

—*Elbert Hubbard*

◇ ◇ ◇

It is far better to admit ignorance than to display it.

◇ ◇ ◇

Everybody is ignorant, only on different subjects.

IMPATIENCE
Impatience has an imp at the beginning of it.

IMPORTANCE
Some men grow; others only swell.

◇   ◇   ◇

The size of a person can be judged by the issues he advocates.

◇   ◇   ◇

It is much more important to be human than to be important.

◇   ◇   ◇

Every Christian is "somebody." He has a calling. He is a disciple, a witness, a believer, a brother, a Christian.

◇   ◇   ◇

The most important things are eternal.

◇   ◇   ◇

A great many important people say some very unimportant things.

IMPOSSIBILITY
Only he who can see the Invisible can do the impossible.
—*"War Cry"*

◇   ◇   ◇

When you try the impossible, you test the resources of God.

◇   ◇   ◇

Never think a task is impossible just because you think so.

◇   ◇   ◇

A fellow who says it can't be done is likely to be interrupted by someone doing it.

IMPROVEMENT

The largest room in all the world is for improvement.

◇   ◇   ◇

You may not be able to remake yourself but you can always make the best use of what God gave you to work with.

INDUSTRIOUSNESS

Let not your left hand know what your right hand is doing, but be sure it is doing something.

◇   ◇   ◇

Every morning tell the man in the mirror, "Today I am going to do good work."

◇   ◇   ◇

If you make it a habit to lean on others, you may expect some lean years.

◇   ◇   ◇

It is a great thing to do a small thing well.

◇   ◇   ◇

Hats off to the past; coats off to the future!

◇   ◇   ◇

Industry is a better horse to ride than genius.

◇   ◇   ◇

If a man would move the world, he must first move himself.

◇   ◇   ◇

Everything comes to him who hustles while he waits.

—*Thomas A. Edison*

◇   ◇   ◇

It is easier to keep up than to catch up.

◇   ◇   ◇

It may be true that the willing horse gets the heaviest load, but he also develops the strongest muscles and generally gets the most oats.

150

INFLUENCE

The depth of one's conviction measures the breadth of one's influence.

◇ ◇ ◇

General Motors discovered that the average person has a strong influence on at least 162 people during his life.

◇ ◇ ◇

You cannot always convince people by argument or by your testimony, but you can make them hungry for what you've got.

◇ ◇ ◇

Christianity is not always taught; frequently it is caught.

◇ ◇ ◇

H. R. L. Sheppard, a British preacher, tells of losing his faith because as a college undergraduate he had seen a bishop unable to take a beating at tennis like a gentleman.

◇ ◇ ◇

Does love in every handclasp flow in sympathy's caress?
Do those that I have greeted know a newborn hopefulness?
Are tolerance and charity the keynote of my song as I go plodding onward with earth's eager, anxious throng?

—Strickland Gillilan

INVESTMENT

Goodness is one investment that never fails.

◇ ◇ ◇

Spiritual investments bring the greatest dividends.

JEALOUSY

Jealousy is the fine art of the small soul.

151

JESUS CHRIST

The depths of Christ are unsearchable. The love of Christ passeth knowledge. The grace of Christ is immeasurable. The glory of Christ is unfathomable. There are deeps beyond deep, heights beyond height. Deep calls unto deep, and glory unto glory. To the natural man they are without meaning; to the taught of the Spirit they are eternally sure.

—*Samuel Chadwick*

◇　◇　◇

The earliest confession of faith: "Jesus is Lord."

◇　◇　◇

I have looked far and wide, inside and outside my own head and heart, and I have found nothing other than this Man and His words which offers any answer to the dilemmas of this tragic, troubled time. If His light has gone out, then, as far as I am concerned, there is no light.

—*Malcolm Muggeridge*

◇　◇　◇

The teachings of Christ are wholly contrary to the beliefs of the modern world. The spiritual philosophy underlying the kingdom of God is radically opposed to that of civilized society. In short, the Christ of the New Testament and the world of mankind are so sharply opposed to each other as to amount to downright hostility. To achieve a compromise is impossible.

◇　◇　◇

Jesus is the Christ of the distressed, the Comforter of him who sorrows, the Burden Bearer, the Hope of the one who has failed. But He comes again when the skies are bright, when successful effort draws toward the goal, and demands of us, "Lovest thou me more than these?"

—*Charles A. McConnell*

◇　◇　◇

152

After 19 centuries Jesus is still the disturbing, surprising, fascinating Master of men. Even skeptics cannot get Him out of their minds. He has a tremendous, almost irresistible appeal to all races and classes.

—*Massey M. Heltzel*

◊   ◊   ◊

You are complete in Christ only when you are completely in Christ.

◊   ◊   ◊

Christ is not valued at all unless He is valued above all.

—*St. Augustine*

◊   ◊   ◊

Christ came not to make life easy but to make men great.

◊   ◊   ◊

Christ can meet
Each human need.
Christ can satisfy
Indeed!

◊   ◊   ◊

Christ's limitless resources meet our endless needs.

◊   ◊   ◊

Christ went about doing good; many of us are content just going about.

◊   ◊   ◊

People say that Jesus Christ came to teach us to be good. He never did! All the teaching in the world about a man having a pure heart won't make it pure. Our Lord's teaching has no power in it unless I possess His nature.

—*Oswald Chambers*

◊   ◊   ◊

Jesus Christ based all His teaching on the fundamental

fact that God can do for a man what a man cannot do for himself.

—*Oswald Chambers*

◇　◇　◇

Without Christ our past would be unpardonable, our present would be intolerable, our future would be impenetrable.

◇　◇　◇

My gypsy tent, if Jesus be in it, is as grand as St. Paul's Cathedral, and St. Paul's Cathedral is nothing but a glorified quarry without Jesus. Christ makes the temple.

—*Gypsy Smith*

◇　◇　◇

He is Light in darkness, Joy in sadness, Riches in poverty, Life in death. It is He who can resolve all your doubts, secure you in danger, save your soul, and bring you to glory where all joys are full.

◇　◇　◇

The fullness of heaven is Jesus himself;
The duration of heaven is the eternity of Jesus;
The light of heaven is the face of Jesus;
The joy of heaven is the presence of Jesus;
The melody of heaven is the songs of praise to Jesus;
The harmony of heaven is the fellowship of Jesus;
The theme of heaven is the glory of Jesus;
The employment of heaven is the worship of Jesus.

◇　◇　◇

Jesus was more than a great moral Teacher; he was more than a Pattern for us to follow. He was the eternal Son of God, incarnated in human flesh. This is the distinctive doctrine of the Christian religion.

◇　◇　◇

He was the Son of God, thinking out to man.
He was the heart of God, throbbing out to man.

154

He was the voice of God, calling out to man.

He was the hand of God, strong and tender, reaching out to man.

He was the person of God, wearing human attire and living in a humble carpenter shop.

All this that He might find man and take him back to God.

—*Bishop Arthur Moore*

◇　◇　◇

Jesus is the supreme need in peace or storm.

◇　◇　◇

Christ is the Way; why waste time traveling any other?

◇　◇　◇

Jesus was strong, winsome, gentle, good with the very goodness of God, yearning after the welfare of human beings, concerned that both body and soul should have a fair chance, opposed to all the hurts and harms of human life.

◇　◇　◇

Thou dost turn the darkness into light, the desert into a garden, our sin into holiness, our sorrow into rejoicing, our weeping into laughter, our despair into hope, our despondency into joy, our defeat into victory, our turmoil into peace, our fears into faith, our doubts into assurance.

◇　◇　◇

The glory of Christ can transform your life, turning your darkness into day; casting your sins into the sea of His forgetfulness; hallowing the routine, the humdrum into the inspired; investing the ordinary, the commonplace with the glow of His presence.

◇　◇　◇

When a person gets a good look at Jesus Christ the Lord, he will never be the same man again.

◇　◇　◇

If Christ is left outside, something is wrong inside.

◇　◇　◇

No one needs the saving mercy of Christ so much as the person who thinks merely of saving himself.

◇　◇　◇

There is no man in all the world whom Jesus Christ does not understand.

◇　◇　◇

Are you portraying Christ or betraying Him?

◇　◇　◇

Christ died for you; are you living for Him?

◇　◇　◇

God said, Let us FORM man in our image.
The world says: We must CONFORM man to our image.
The devil says: I will DEFORM man by sin.
Education says: Let us INFORM man by knowledge.
Society says: We will REFORM man by culture.
Christ says: I will TRANSFORM man by love.

◇　◇　◇

The words "Believe on the Lord Jesus Christ" really mean "to have an absolute personal reliance upon the Lord Jesus Christ as Saviour."

◇　◇　◇

"In Christ"! This favorite phrase of Paul's is absent in only one letter—2 Thessalonians. It is not so much the essence of Paul's theology as it is the summary of his whole religion.

◇　◇　◇

Love Christ with all your heart and do as you please.

—*St. Augustine*

JOY

Joy is much more than happiness. It is exultation of spirit, says the dictionary: gladness, delight, a state of felicity. Awe and a sense of mystery are part of it. So are the feelings of humility and gratitude.

◇   ◇   ◇

Our strength is more than rugged convictions, high ideals, or grim determination. It is as true today as it was when the words were penned, "The joy of the Lord is your strength."

◇   ◇   ◇

Fun is natural pleasure; joy is spiritual pleasure.

◇   ◇   ◇

Joy is discovered in the change, conflict, disturbance, loss, and confusion which often make others unhappy. Joy is unassailable, untouchable, undisturbable. Joy is the outward manifestation of the inner experience of grace.

◇   ◇   ◇

A missing note in the Church today is best summed up in one small word. It is the word *joy*. There is no lack of orthodoxy. There is no shortage of moral ruggedness. We have a good degree of conscientiousness and dependability. But we lack radiance, the contagious quality of joy.

◇   ◇   ◇

Whatever the defeats of the moment, the lost skirmishes of the day, the final victory is sure. The joy of God does not deny the tears. It looks through and beyond them to "the day without a cloud."

—"Herald of Holiness"

◇   ◇   ◇

Joy which we cannot share with others is only half enjoyed.

◇   ◇   ◇

Joy is something that is multiplied when it is divided.

◇   ◇   ◇

157

To be joyful in our jobs, we must give joy to others in their jobs.

JUDGING

A friend is one who waits about passing judgment until he has heard what we have to say in our own defense.

◇   ◇   ◇

It is not always safe to judge a man by his relatives.

KINDNESS

You can repay a loan, but you are forever in debt to those who are kind.

◇   ◇   ◇

Learn to say kind things. Nobody ever resents them.

◇   ◇   ◇

The milk of human kindness never curdles.

◇   ◇   ◇

To be polite is to do and say the kindest thing in the kindest way.

◇   ◇   ◇

Life without industry is guilt. Industry without art is brutality.

◇   ◇   ◇

A kindness loses its grace by being noised abroad.

◇   ◇   ◇

Be kind! Every person you meet is fighting a difficult battle.

KNOWLEDGE

Action is the proper fruit of knowledge.

◇   ◇   ◇

Imagination is more important than knowledge.

◇   ◇   ◇

158

The man who knows it all has no use for God.

◇ ◇ ◇

Half knowledge is worse than ignorance.

◇ ◇ ◇

Some students drink at the fountain of knowledge. Others just gargle.

◇ ◇ ◇

You do not have to be listed in *Who's Who* to know what's what.

◇ ◇ ◇

Knowledge is vain and fruitless which is not reduced to practice.

—*Matthew Henry*

LAUGHTER

It is one of the anomalies of our day that, while civilization trembles at the possibility of destruction, the American people spend more time than ever laughing themselves to death. While hospitals are crowded with nervous and mental wrecks; while suicide, crime, broken homes, and delinquency set records, television clowns are paid fortunes to amuse us night after night, turning tragedy into comedy. Never in history has there been more ribald hilarity with less to be funny about. This attitude has spilled over into religion.

—*Vance Havner*

◇ ◇ ◇

Take time to laugh. It is the music of the soul.

◇ ◇ ◇

Learn to laugh. It's better than medicine.

◇ ◇ ◇

He who laughs, lasts.

159

LAZINESS

Following the line of least resistance makes rivers and men crooked.

◇　◇　◇

Indecision is often a lack of energy.

◇　◇　◇

Some people get along with others by throwing their minds into neutral and going where they are pushed.

◇　◇　◇

The fellow who does as he pleases is seldom pleased with what he does.

◇　◇　◇

The man who falls down needs to be helped up. The man who lies down needs to be punched.

◇　◇　◇

I know some people who not only believe the world owes them a living, but are conceited enough to think that they are preferred creditors.

◇　◇　◇

I have never yet seen an outstretched hand with the palm upward that had a callous on it.

LEADERSHIP

To be a leader, learn to face the music.

◇　◇　◇

No leader can go forward any faster than the people will follow.

LIMITATIONS

A man's real limitations are not the things he wants to do and cannot; they are the things he ought to do but does not.

160

LIFE

Spend your life for something that outlasts it.

◇ ◇ ◇

When life is all tangled up and you can't find your way out, go to church.

◇ ◇ ◇

Life must be measured by its quality, not by its length.

◇ ◇ ◇

Life is a trust from God.

◇ ◇ ◇

Some men make a living; others make a life.

◇ ◇ ◇

A life is beautiful only as it is useful and helpful.

◇ ◇ ◇

We make a living by what we get, but we make a life by what we give.

◇ ◇ ◇

There is nothing in life that is beyond the concern of good religion.

◇ ◇ ◇

The Word of God gives life wherever it is received.

◇ ◇ ◇

Life is far too short to be little.

◇ ◇ ◇

To many of us, life is a process of getting used to things we hadn't expected.

◇ ◇ ◇

Life is hard by the yard; but by the inch, it's a cinch.

◇ ◇ ◇

Life without purpose is life without interest.

◇ ◇ ◇

Life's supreme act is walking with God.

◇ ◇ ◇

If you would get life's best, see to it that life gets your best.

◇   ◇   ◇

Until life begins with God it does not begin.

◇   ◇   ◇

Put work into your life and life into your work.

◇   ◇   ◇

Life is a one-way street and we are not coming back.

◇   ◇   ◇

Life is like a ladder; every step we take is either up or down.

—*Roger Babson*

◇   ◇   ◇

Your life is 10 percent what you make it, 90 percent how you take it.

◇   ◇   ◇

Life is tragic for those who have plenty to live on and nothing to live for.

LIVING

It is difficult to live in the present, ridiculous to live in the future, and impossible to live in the past. Nothing is as far away as one minute ago.

—*Jim Bishop*

◇   ◇   ◇

The scholar has learned how to think; the wise man has learned how to live.

◇   ◇   ◇

The first step in learning to live is submitting to the will of God.

◇   ◇   ◇

The strongest principle of growth lies in human choice.

◇   ◇   ◇

I expect to pass through this world but once. Any good thing, therefore, I can do, or any kindness I can show to any fellow human being, let me do it now. Let me not defer nor neglect it, for I shall not pass this way again.

—*Stephen Grellet*

◇　◇　◇

Few men ever outlive their desire to be better than they are.

◇　◇　◇

Better a little "taffy" while they live than so much "epitaphy" when they are dead.

◇　◇　◇

Pay no attention to ill-natured remarks about you. Live so that nobody will believe them.

◇　◇　◇

It is more to one's credit to go straight than to move in the best circles.

◇　◇　◇

Live to make life less difficult for others.

◇　◇　◇

If they could just see themselves as others see them, I know a lot of folks would change their way of living.

◇　◇　◇

It matters not how long we live, but how.

◇　◇　◇

Right living is a whole lot better than high living and a lot cheaper.

◇　◇　◇

Are you conducting your life on the cafeteria plan—self-service only?

◇　◇　◇

You can make the world better by making yourself better.

◇　◇　◇

I'll live today. I'll carry today's burdens; I'll give today my best service, my happiest smile, and live all the day through.

⋄ ⋄ ⋄

Today is ours. Let's live it.

⋄ ⋄ ⋄

Do your best today and then do better tomorrow.

⋄ ⋄ ⋄

The common verities of daily life include joy and sorrow.

⋄ ⋄ ⋄

Love, kindness, forgiveness may be reflected in our everyday living.

⋄ ⋄ ⋄

> *The past is gone—*
> *Don't rue it.*
> *The future vast—*
> *Don't fear it.*
> *Today is ours—*
> *Let's live it.*

⋄ ⋄ ⋄

The supreme art of life is that of living together justly, happily, charitably, and nobly.

⋄ ⋄ ⋄

The few days that God gives us are too precious to be trifled with.

⋄ ⋄ ⋄

Live a life; do not only get a living.

⋄ ⋄ ⋄

Some people know all about how to make a living, but very little about how to live.

LONELINESS

It is easy to see that a man without God and His Word is an empty person, that he is lonely, confused, and insecure in his heart. I met a man in an old log house on the Blue Ridge Mountains who knew God. He read a Bible with stained pages by a kerosene lamp and he had a full life. I met a man in Pittsburgh who had wealth, power, prestige, and was an alcoholic. He had no contact with God; he was empty, bitter, and lonely, and finally committed suicide.

—William Goodman

◇ ◇ ◇

The Christian must walk on a lonesome way. It takes courage and conviction to go against a crowd, to stand alone. It is not pleasant to be misunderstood and misinterpreted. A Christian in a non-Christian society must be a nonconformist. This will often put him out in bold relief. He must be willing to "stick his neck out"; to risk discomfort, reputation, freedom, and even life itself for the sake of truth and right.

◇ ◇ ◇

Life is not beautiful all the time. But through the ugliness and pain and agony and loneliness there is available to every human being the fragrance of the very Presence of Christ.

—Eugenia Price

◇ ◇ ◇

I never get lonely, because I am never alone.

◇ ◇ ◇

To know how to be alone and not be lonely is the sum of wisdom and of religion.

THE LORD'S DAY

Saturday has no sorrow that Sunday cannot heal—if Sunday is a day of worship, prayer, and praise.

◇ ◇ ◇

More is said about the fourth commandment than about any other. Only four words were needed in regard to kill-

165

ing: "Thou shalt not kill." But 94 words were used to tell us to "remember the sabbath day, to keep it holy."

◇ ◇ ◇

Keep your Sundays for the great things of the soul.

◇ ◇ ◇

Buying even an ice-cream cone was once taboo on Sunday. Now Christians are seen standing in line at restaurants waiting for their Sunday dinners. Women say it's much easier on them if they go out to eat. Who ever said Sunday dinner had to be a big, long-worked-over meal, anyway? Many could do with less eating and profit by it.

—Donna Litherland

◇ ◇ ◇

The Bible tells us that in the last days there will be a falling away. Men will seek after pleasure—money, eating, prosperity, fleshly satisfaction—more than after God. This trend toward desecrating the Sabbath day may be one more indication that we are living in the last times. Let us not be part of that falling away.

—Donna Litherland

◇ ◇ ◇

Voltaire was once asked, "How can Christianity be destroyed?" His answer was "By destroying the Christian Sabbath."

◇ ◇ ◇

Many a Christian's low standards of the observance of the Lord's Day can be characterized as "the tragedy of being trapped by trivia."

◇ ◇ ◇

Proper observance of the Lord's Day helps to make worship more meaningful, makes us conscious of God, helps to develop an awareness of spiritual things.

◇ ◇ ◇

166

One of the most terrifying symptoms of spiritual decline in our day is the Christian's careless Sundays.

◇ ◇ ◇

Monday to Saturday is the test of Sunday.

◇ ◇ ◇

For the early Christians the Sabbath became the first day of the week in commemoration of the fact that Jesus rose from the dead on the first day of the week. This made the day holy. It had a divine meaning in the weekly message of resurrection. It was appropriate that the holiness of the old Jewish Sabbath be transferred to the Christian first-day observance.

◇ ◇ ◇

In a materialistic, secularistic, irreligious age such as ours unquestionably is, the commandments say to us, even as they said to the Hebrews, "Make room for God in your daily life. And set aside one day in seven for His glory."

◇ ◇ ◇

There may be nothing actually wrong or harmful in certain forms of activity on the Lord's Day. But the point is: What is right in doing this or that? Is it the best thing to do? Does doing this or that contribute to the highest spiritual well-being of myself and others?

◇ ◇ ◇

The Lord's Day should be a day dedicated to God; a day, not only of assembling in God's house, but one of withdrawing as much as possible from the world, of heart searching, of renewal, of strengthening the sinews of our spiritual being for the conflicts of the coming week.

◇ ◇ ◇

There is probably no more accurate test of one's Christian devotion than one's attitude toward and conduct on the Lord's Day.

◇ ◇ ◇

167

A Christian's carelessness in observing Sunday as a day of rest and worship betrays a callousness to Bible standards.

◇ ◇ ◇

A hearse is a poor vehicle in which to ride to church. Why wait for it?

◇ ◇ ◇

Some men never think of economizing on gasoline except on Sunday morning.

◇ ◇ ◇

A desecration of the Sabbath means a blow at the entire structure of faith.

◇ ◇ ◇

The Sunday morning church bell tolls the spiritual death of the member who does not come.

◇ ◇ ◇

Seven days without Christ makes one weak.

◇ ◇ ◇

The Sabbath is a firm foundation on which to build a six-story week.

◇ ◇ ◇

Our Sabbath days are quiet islands in the tossing sea of life.

◇ ◇ ◇

Sunday should mean more than eating a choice dinner or putting on your best clothes.

◇ ◇ ◇

No Christian can keep the faith and not keep the Sabbath.

◇ ◇ ◇

A world without a Sabbath would be like a man without a smile, like a summer without flowers, and like a homestead without a garden. It is the joyous day of the whole week.

—*Henry Ward Beecher*

LOVE

Love that is hoarded molds at last,
Until we know someday
The only things we ever have
Are those we give away.

◇   ◇   ◇

The sure test of love is the length to which it will go.

◇   ◇   ◇

Love speaks all languages.

◇   ◇   ◇

Love never reaches satiety.

◇   ◇   ◇

An ounce of charity is better than a pound of sympathy.

◇   ◇   ◇

Faith—gets the most.
Humility—keeps the most.
Love—works the most.

◇   ◇   ◇

Love and you shall be loved.

◇   ◇   ◇

Love that doesn't understand the language of sacrifice is not love.

◇   ◇   ◇

To be loved, one must be lovable and must love.

—Benjamin Franklin

◇   ◇   ◇

"Love," said one girl, "is the funny feeling that you feel when you feel that you have a feeling you never felt before."

◇   ◇   ◇

Love never asks, "How much must I do?" but, "How much can I do?"

◇   ◇   ◇

169

Perfect love is slow to demand, quick to give.

◇ ◇ ◇

Loving the unlovely is the test of love.

◇ ◇ ◇

When love comes from within, it is reflected in our thoughts and deeds.

◇ ◇ ◇

Love makes the burden of life lighter.

◇ ◇ ◇

Love is never genuine unless it is willing to suffer.

◇ ◇ ◇

The true opposite of love is not hate but indifference. Hate, bad as it is, at least treats the neighbor as a "thou," whereas indifference turns the neighbor into an "it," a thing.

—Joseph Fletcher

◇ ◇ ◇

If we discovered that we had only five minutes left to say all we wanted to say, every telephone booth would be occupied by people calling other people to stammer that they loved them.

—Christopher Morley

◇ ◇ ◇

The world needs love; people's lives have been blighted by love starvation.

◇ ◇ ◇

Love was never more indispensable, more necessary to the sanity of humanity than now. When the chips are down, we all fall back to that simple affirmation "What the world needs now is love."

◇ ◇ ◇

If we can love enough, this is the touchstone. Love is the medicine for the sickness of the world.

—Karl Menninger

◇ ◇ ◇

With but few exceptions, all psychoneurotic symptoms can be traced to one common cause—deprivation of love.

—*Leslie Weatherhead*

◇　◇　◇

Do you know someone who has despitefully used you? Someone who hates you? Someone who has wrongly judged you? Someone who has betrayed a trust? Such a one is a great challenge and opportunity for you. Such a one is a perfect person for you to love.

◇　◇　◇

We are shaped and fashioned by what we love.

—*Goethe*

◇　◇　◇

To be manifestly loved, to be openly admired, are human needs as basic as breathing. Why, then, wanting them so much ourselves, do we deny them so often to others?

◇　◇　◇

To be manifestly loved, to be openly admired, are human needs as basic as breathing. Why, then, wanting them so much ourselves, do we deny them so often to others?

◇　◇　◇

If we were all perfect, there would be no need of love in the world.

◇　◇　◇

Love is affectionate interest.

◇　◇　◇

God remembers our labors of love.

◇　◇　◇

How do we react to unlovely persons? With contempt, scorn, disgust, or with compassion, pity, love, patience (endurance)? Never forget that the test of love is the length to which it will go.

◇　◇　◇

One loving heart sets another on fire.

◇ ◇ ◇

Once I knew the depth where no hope was, and darkness lay on the face of all things. Then love came and set my soul free. Once I fretted and beat myself against the wall that shut me in. My life was without a past or a future, and death a consummation devoutly to be wished. But a little word from the fingers of another fell into my hands that clutched at emptiness, and my heart leaped up with the rapture of living.

—*Helen Keller*

◇ ◇ ◇

A spirit of love and earnest prayer will not solve all problems nor erase all differences, but it will favorably affect the outcome of any situation.

◇ ◇ ◇

God's love to me is inexhaustible, and I must love others from the bedrock of God's love to me.

◇ ◇ ◇

It is time for a great revival of love among the people called the holy people. We need a love that rejects gossip, that scorns slander, that is manifest in words of encouragement, in deeds of kindness and sympathetic understanding.

—*Oliver G. Wilson*

◇ ◇ ◇

Sociology says, "Respect all humanity"; but Christ says, "Love thy neighbour."

◇ ◇ ◇

Love, like light, shines on, however it may be received. Men may hate it, but love continues. Men may get so hardened as not to be influenced by it, but God loves them still. Men may persecute and injure and rebel against and hate those who love them, but these things cannot destroy

172

the love. Love is like the laws of nature; you may break them but they continue operating.

◇ ◇ ◇

The deepest need of man is the need to overcome his separateness, to leave the prison of his aloneness. The full answer to the problem of existence lies in true and mature love.

—*Erich Fromm*

◇ ◇ ◇

Let your love wrap itself around those you come in contact with each day, and at the end of the day you will say that life has been wonderful.

◇ ◇ ◇

Love is not basically emotional. Love is not sentimentality. Love is a deliberate, voluntary, profound, practical, earthy dedication of the whole self to the Lord Jesus Christ.

◇ ◇ ◇

Someday, after mastering the winds, the waves, the tides, and gravity, we shall harness for God the energies of love, and then, for the second time in the history of the world, man will discover fire.

—*Teilhard de Chardin*

◇ ◇ ◇

Love occurs 60 times in John's Gospel, 46 times in three chapters of First John.

◇ ◇ ◇

Christian love is not soft and gullible, easily taken in. It is not blind to another's faults or sins. But it insists on looking through the hard crust, the crude manners, the nasty tempers, the evil habits—searching for something to believe in.

◇ ◇ ◇

Love bridges the culture gap—whether between individuals of different races or between educated and illiterate,

173

prosperous and poor. Love bridges the communication gap. It speaks "between the lines" and adds overtones to words that without love would be gibberish to the other person. Love bridges the credibility gap. The love of God is believeable usually only when it is reflected from the life of another person. Love, they say, is blind. Better it would be to say that love is blind to the things that do not really matter, and very farsighted in regard to the things that do matter.

—W. T. Purkiser

◇   ◇   ◇

The test of Christian discipleship is not orthodoxy of belief, correctness of conduct, or earnestness of effort to extend the Kingdom. "By this shall all men know that ye are my disciples, if ye have love one to another."

◇   ◇   ◇

Love feels no burden, regards not labors, would willingly do more than it is able, pleads not impossibilities, because it feels sure that it can and may do all things. Love is swift, sincere, pious, pleasant, and strong; patient, faithful, prudent, longsuffering, manly, and never seeking itself; it is circumspect, humble, and upright; sober, chaste, steadfast, quiet, and guarded in all its senses.

—Thomas a Kempis

◇   ◇   ◇

Our love for Christ must be able to stand foul odors and loathsome sights, so that we will go down to the gates of hell to save a lost soul.

—Arthur J. Moore

◇   ◇   ◇

We never know what is lying dormant in the dry soil of a sinner's love-starved personality. So by your trust and confidence and love you fertilize the soil and create the

174

emotional climate in which those neglected seeds of character can grow.

◇ ◇ ◇

When you can bear all things, believe all things, hope all things, endure all things, in your relationships with your friends, your neighbors, your fellow church members, your family, and 'yourself, then rejoice and take heart, for you are following in the footsteps of your Lord.

◇ ◇ ◇

It is not always easy, in the midst of pressing circumstances, to lose ourselves in the needs of others. One of the grandest sights on earth is to see a servant of God ministering to the needs of others, all unconscious of his own needs.

◇ ◇ ◇

Loving others is not always easy because it must be continuous, not spasmodic, not by moods or impulses. There are no moments, hours, days, that do not count.

◇ ◇ ◇

Christian love is the lubricant that helps people to live together without too much friction.

◇ ◇ ◇

Jesus did not leave a system of ethics, nor a list of rules, nor a program of religious activities, nor a theology. But He did leave one great, all-inclusive principle of action wrapped up in the word *LOVE*.

◇ ◇ ◇

The great commandment of the New Testament makes a unified personality—no conflict, no cross-purposes, no double-mindedness. It puts one fundamental command in place of 10; it gives us one spot to watch. It says, "Keep the fountain, the source, pure." It allows for one

175

concern and only one. It reduces all of life to a single ruling motive—LOVE. Simple, isn't it!

◇ ◇ ◇

Christian love is patient and kind. This doesn't mean spinelessness and want of courage. Jesus was relentless. Christ loves us with a love that never lets us go and never lets us off.

◇ ◇ ◇

Love is a moving, creating, healing power of life and unites life with life, person with person, and is not easily discouraged.

◇ ◇ ◇

It would be powerfully strange if Christians ever became Christians in the full sense of love. The uncommitted millions of the world, and thousands in America, would be overwhelmed by such a sight. They might even take our Christianity seriously if we did.

◇ ◇ ◇

Love—the four-dimensional grace:
Love—the unbreakable grace, "Beareth all things."
Love—the unsuspicious grace, "Believeth all things."
Love—the optimistic grace, "Hopeth all things."
Love—the tenacious grace, "Endureth all things."

—H. K. Bedwell

◇ ◇ ◇

"I have not used the word *love* in the last three years," a young minister said. "It's too dangerous. No one knows what it means! I refer only to concern, respect, and affectionate appreciation."

◇ ◇ ◇

God loved me when I was unlovable, vile and contemptible, and full of sin. How far do I need to go before I show the same love to others? Before I fully measure up to Jesus' command: "Love as I have love you."

◇ ◇ ◇

They went about their lives quietly, singing hymns; not yet preoccupied by thoughts of a stable Church and ecclesiastical institutions, obeying the new law announced by Jesus, in compassionate love for one another. Love was the law, celebrated in the love feast and whenever the brethren came together.

◇　◇　◇

Many a person has been lost to Christ and the Church by a religion that is stern, grim, inflexible, legalistic, domineering, but without love.

◇　◇　◇

Love shrinks from the ugly and offensive, but it overcomes and loves all the more for the greater need.

—*Samuel Chadwick*

◇　◇　◇

Seek out the one who is filled with hate and misery, the one who is mean and contemptible and unlovely. Love him until his heart melts and he receives the healing, cleansing love of God which is flowing through you.

◇　◇　◇

What frequently passes for love can be greedy, selfish, tyrannical, demanding. True love does not cling, hurt, or drain. It strengthens, supports, heals.

◇　◇　◇

> *If I can stop one heart from breaking,*
> *I shall not live in vain;*
> *If I can ease one life the aching,*
> *Or cool one pain,*
> *Or help one fainting robin*
> *Unto his nest again,*
> *I shall not live in vain.*

—*Emily Dickinson*

◇　◇　◇

All religions offer a way of life and a way into eternity. Greek philosophy said, "Know thyself." Confucianism says, "Correct thyself." Islam says, "Assert thyself." Ancient Rome said, "Express thyself." Judaism says, "Conform thyself." But Christianity says, "Deny thyself." The last is the act of love.

◇ ◇ ◇

Loving God is not always easy, because it must be inclusive. There is no partial redemption; there can be no partial love. It is all or nothing. The great commandment requires that a man is: heart, mind, soul, strength.

◇ ◇ ◇

Love watcheth, and sleeping, it sleepeth not. Being tired, is not weary; straitened, is not pressed; frightened, but not disturbed; but like a lively flame it bursteth out aloft and securely passeth through all.

—Thomas a Kempis

◇ ◇ ◇

The true Christian labors in love, speaks the language of love, dips mercy with the ladle of love, yearns for the lost with lamentations of love, seeks the straying with the lantern of love, and draws men with the lariat of love.

◇ ◇ ◇

What one lives for practically determines the philosophy he has chosen:

    Money—then materialism
    Power—then force
    Popularity—then compromise
    Pleasure—then self-indulgence
    Jesus and love—then self-forgetfulness

◇ ◇ ◇

Love is an absolute requirement in the Kingdom which Jesus brought in. Christians are known for their love of one another. How is the Christian really different from the cultured, respectable, and upright persons around him? It is the quality of love, a love without sham, a love without pride and condescension.

◇　◇　◇

Men will fight for Christianity and die for Christianity but not live in its spirit, which is love. It is always possible to human nature to make sacrifices and engage in arduous duties. The impossible thing is love. It cannot be worked up. It is the result of God entering and possessing the soul.

◇　◇　◇

Love, like faith, is a gift from God. It is impossible to split up love into fragments, with some extended to God and some withheld from man.

◇　◇　◇

Faith makes things possible, and love makes them easy.

◇　◇　◇

"I was that stranger," says the Master. "I was that homeless child. I was the gas station attendant, the waiter in the restaurant, the clerk in that store. Would you have treated them any differently if you had known?"

—*Donald H. Strong*

◇　◇　◇

The Bible is unique in its complexity and its simplicity. It touches every century, speaks of every subject, and contains advice and guidance on every problem. Yet all its commands may be narrowed down to two, and those two may be summarized in one word, *love*. Henry Drummond rightly called love "the greatest thing in the world."

—*Donald H. Strong*

◇　◇　◇

Slowly, surely, love melts icicles of opposition, wears down walls of indifference, opens long-closed doors into the hearts of others. How we need the gentle, warming, healing balm of love to mend broken families and to repair fractured friendships!

—*Donald H. Strong*

◇   ◇   ◇

God is love, love is life, and life is eternal.

◇   ◇   ◇

Love is centered in God. Love is manifested in Christ. Love should be exemplified in and through His followers.

◇   ◇   ◇

Christianity is the only religion whose Deity seeks man. That is love!

◇   ◇   ◇

May the shining of Thy love drive the shadows from our lives, making them centers of health, cheerfulness, and courage. Light the flame of faith upon the altars of our minds. Help us to praise Thee with lives of radiant outreach and selfless service. May we go forth with love toward all men, imparting hope to the discouraged, with support to the weak, and with the water of life to the multitudes dying with thirst!

◇   ◇   ◇

God in His love hurts that He may heal. Often our distress is a prelude to seeking God.

◇   ◇   ◇

Love is the last word in religion. It completes the revelation of God and sums up the whole duty of man. Love is of God, and the Spirit of God is the Spirit of love.

—*Samuel Chadwick*

◇   ◇   ◇

When once you realize all that it cost God to forgive you, you will be held as in a vise, constrained by the love of God.

—*Oswald Chambers*

◇   ◇   ◇

In Thy presence we forget our limitations and reach beyond ourselves to the realm of Thy limitless power. In Thy presence we find rest; in Thy wisdom we find truth; in Thy mercy we find forgiveness; in Thy love we find an answer to the evil and suffering in the world.

LUCK

I am a great believer in luck. Funny thing about it, however, is that the harder I work, the more luck I seem to have.

◊ ◊ ◊

Being everlastingly on the job beats carrying a rabbit's foot.

◊ ◊ ◊

The best substitute for luck is ambition.

LYING

The biggest liar in the world is the Christian who gives excuses for not doing his duty.

◊ ◊ ◊

You can look and act a lie just as effectively as telling one.

◊ ◊ ◊

"Somebody told me" is often the beginning of a lie.

◊ ◊ ◊

Those who are given to white lies soon become color blind.

MAJORITY

One man with courage makes a majority.

◊ ◊ ◊

One plus God equals a majority.

MARRIAGE

Intuition is the strange instinct that tells a woman she is right whether she is or not.

◇ ◇ ◇

A wife who keeps the corners of her mouth up and her voice down has her problem half solved.

◇ ◇ ◇

An important factor in maintaining a happy home is the light touch. Learn to handle irritations lightly. A little flattery, a humorous approach helps.

◇ ◇ ◇

Try praising your wife. It may frighten her a little at first, but try it.

◇ ◇ ◇

Keeping your husband in hot water makes him hard-boiled, not tender.

◇ ◇ ◇

The more dishwater the wedding ring sees, the longer it seems to last.

MEMORY

A memory stored with scripture is a bank that will never fail.

MIND

If a man thinks wrongly, he will live wrongly.

◇ ◇ ◇

Great minds have purposes; others have wishes.

◇ ◇ ◇

It is well to remember that open-mindedness is not the same as empty-mindedness.

◇ ◇ ◇

Why is it fellows with the narrowest minds always seem to have the widest mouths?

◇ ◇ ◇

The less they have of it, the more people seem obsessed with the inclination to speak their mind.

◇ ◇ ◇

Keeping an open mind is sometimes a very painful process.

◇ ◇ ◇

Some minds are like concrete: thoroughly mixed and permanently set.

◇ ◇ ◇

As a hollow building echoes all sounds, so a vacant mind is open to all suggestions.

◇ ◇ ◇

The mind is like a parachute. It functions only when it's open.

◇ ◇ ◇

The hardest thing to open is a closed mind.

◇ ◇ ◇

Your mind is as old as Adam and as young as your latest thought.

◇ ◇ ◇

To the average man any question is like the moon—he sees only one side of it.

◇ ◇ ◇

It never pays to argue with a man who is unwilling to be convinced.

◇ ◇ ◇

After watching all manner of salesmen at work, Robert R. Updegraff is convinced that most of them talk too much and too fast, leaving out of their selling the magic ingredient—silence. It is safe to assume that most people's minds work slowly, especially on any new proposition. (*Ed. note:* We might do well to consider this when dealing with souls, as well.)

MISSIONS

The impact of our gospel on the world will be in direct proportion to the velocity, the urgency, with which it is delivered.

—*Samuel Zwemer*

◇　◇　◇

If you want to follow Jesus, you must follow Him to the ends of the earth, for that is where He is going.

—*Robert E. Speer*

◇　◇　◇

The cries of brothers, sisters, 'round the world
Rise up to deafen all the sounds I know.
The Master tells me to go forth and show
*　His nail-pierced hands—His feet—His wounded side,*
And tell my brothers, sisters, everywhere
*　For them He died.*

—*Mabel Starrett*

◇　◇　◇

The Church exists by mission, as fire exists by burning.

—*Emil Brunner*

◇　◇　◇

The best remedy for a sick church is to put it on a missionary diet.

◇　◇　◇

The world begins next door.

◇　◇　◇

A church with a full treasury ought to give more thought to the missionary cause.

MISTAKES

The man who never makes a mistake never makes anything else.

◇　◇　◇

A mistake is what others make; an error what you commit.

◇　◇　◇

It is not fair to judge a man by his one mistake.

◇　◇　◇

I rarely make the same mistake a second time,
　Which isn't surprising.
For it's a full-time job to make the gorgeous new ones
　I keep devising.

MUSIC

There are three classifications of church music:
    (1) Foot music—stirs physical emotions
    (2) Head music—appeals to artistic taste
    (3) Heart music—points the soul to God

◇　◇　◇

Heaven will be richer through the aeons of eternity because of the use of hymns like "Just as I Am" and "Softly and Tenderly Jesus Is Calling."

MONEY

Just pretending to be rich keeps some people poor.

◇　◇　◇

Some days you can't
Lay up a cent.
Instead of in come,
It out went.
　—A. A. Lattimer

◇　◇　◇

Hard work is the yeast that raises the dough.

◇   ◇   ◇

The love of the right use of money is the root of much good.

◇   ◇   ◇

Dollars go further when accompanied by good sense.

◇   ◇   ◇

Money buys everything except health, happiness, and heaven.

◇   ◇   ◇

More people should learn to tell their dollars where to go instead of asking them where they went.

—*Roger Babson*

◇   ◇   ◇

It's not what you'd do with a million
If riches should e'er be your lot,
But what you are doing at present
With the dollar and a quarter you've got.

◇   ◇   ◇

A man is rich according to what he is, not according to what he has.

◇   ◇   ◇

A man is known by the money he keeps.

◇   ◇   ◇

It hardly pays to give a boy a dollar if he has no sense.

◇   ◇   ◇

Character and cash make a fine combination when yoked together, but sometimes the yoke doesn't hold.

◇   ◇   ◇

A miser is a man who does not realize that he is only a steward of what he falsely calls his own.

◇   ◇   ◇

186

Perhaps one reason the dollar will not do as much for you as it used to do is because you do not want to do as much for the dollar as you used to.

◇　◇　◇

Remember that "dough" begins with "do."

◇　◇　◇

The darkest hour in any man's life is when he sits down to plan how to get money without earning it.

◇　◇　◇

Money is not the measure of the man, but it often is a way of finding out how small he is.

◇　◇　◇

It is said that money talks, and sometimes it offers very damaging testimony.

◇　◇　◇

Money is the most portable shape into which personality can precipitate itself.

◇　◇　◇

There is such a thing as a happy miser; it is one who hangs on to all his friends.

◇　◇　◇

Remember that money is only one form of wealth.

MOTHER'S DAY

What Americans spend on carnations on Mother's Day would feed millions.

◇　◇　◇

Beware lest you remember Mother only one day a year.

◇　◇　◇

My mother's oft-repeated prayer was this one—"And we pray for those in authority, that we may lead a quiet and peaceable life." . . . To this end she lived, and was satisfied that her days were common and ordinary . . . It was not the quiet and peace of doing nothing. It was the opposite. It was the quiet and peace of industry and daily toil. . . . Perhaps the greatest satisfaction of all will be realized in the answer to this prayer my mother prayed each evening: "That we may lead a quiet and peaceable life."

—*G. Lewis VanDyne*

◇　◇　◇

A modern woman in Texas wrote, "I've been a liberated woman for years. Christ set me free."

—*C. William Fisher*

NATURE

Man has become the master of about everything in nature except human nature.

NEGLECT

Neglect can destroy a business, a marriage, a friendship, a soul.

NEIGHBORLINESS

No one is rich enough to do without a neighbor.

◇　◇　◇

You can lighten your own load by bearing your neighbor's burden.

◇　◇　◇

If you have a neighbor that you do not like, get acquainted with him. Who knows? You might like him.

◇　◇　◇

Brightening up the life of someone else will put a fresh shine on your own.

◇　◇　◇

188

The time to look down on your neighbor is when you are bending over to give him a lift.

◇   ◇   ◇

Be charitable. We have to live in the same world with other creatures just like us.

NEW YEAR

Use the Bible as God's Signpost on the New Year's road.

◇   ◇   ◇

In the new year, put first things first.

◇   ◇   ◇

A good motto for the new year is: "God is our Sufficiency."

◇   ◇   ◇

You will get out of the new year what you put into it.

◇   ◇   ◇

New Year's Day is a milestone on the way to eternity.

◇   ◇   ◇

Start the new year today by letting Christ become the Lord of your life.

◇   ◇   ◇

May the Lord's presence for the new year be:
    Above you—to guard (Deut. 4:39)
    Underneath you—to support (Deut. 33:27)
    Behind you—as a rearward (Isa. 52:12)
    Before you—to lead (Isa. 45:2)
    At your right hand—to protect (Ps. 125:2)
    Round about—to shield from storms (Ps. 125:2)
    Within—as Companion and Comforter (Gal. 2:20)

◇   ◇   ◇

If the new year outlook is dark, try the uplook.

OBEDIENCE

When God gives a vision, transact business on that line, no matter what it costs.

—*Oswald Chambers*

◇　◇　◇

Every day, for every one of us, some distant trumpet sounds—but never too faint or too far out for our answer to be: "Wait; I'm coming."

◇　◇　◇

Obedience means marching right on whether we feel it or not.

—*D. L. Moody*

OPINION

The most annoying thing about the standpatter is not his stand, but his patter.

◇　◇　◇

Edwin Markham once said: "There are times when sleep is an opinion."

◇　◇　◇

Don't worry about what other people think of you; worry about what you think of other people.

OPPORTUNITY

Opportunities always look bigger going than coming.

◇　◇　◇

Opportunity doesn't travel on any schedule—you just have to watch for it.

◇　◇　◇

A big man is a little man who makes use of an opportunity.

◇　◇　◇

190

Every opportunity means obligation.

◊   ◊   ◊

Opportunity with ability makes responsibility.

OTHERS

No one can be wrong with man and right with God.

◊   ◊   ◊

If you put *first* communion with God, relationships with other persons become easy and beautifully natural.

—*Bertha Munro*

◊   ◊   ◊

Nothing, except God, is more important than human personality. To appreciate others is to rejoice at their success, to sorrow at their failures, to praise their abilities, to deal kindly although firmly with weaknesses and failures, to sense their aspirations, to respect their rights, and to regard them with warmth and affection.

◊   ◊   ◊

We prove our faith when we reveal God to others. Christ said, "He that hath seen me hath seen the Father." How fragmentary our lives are! How little of God others see in us!

◊   ◊   ◊

The proof of our faith lies in the measure in which we let our hearts feel for others. Do we look upon suffering without suffering? What is the matter with those who profess faith in Christ who see hurt but are not moved? Who see wrong but are not angered? Who see need and are not moved with compassion?

◊   ◊   ◊

"Don't worry" makes a better motto when you add "others."

◊   ◊   ◊

Blessed is the man who does not depend upon other people for his spirit of good humor.

◇   ◇   ◇

We best deal with our wounds when we bring ointment to heal the wounds of others.

◇   ◇   ◇

Indeed, to do the best for others is finally to do the best for ourselves; but it will not do to have our eyes fixed on that issue.

—*John Ruskin*

◇   ◇   ◇

Be what you want others to be.

◇   ◇   ◇

You will never be unemployed if you watch yourself more closely than others.

◇   ◇   ◇

Nothing is eternal but that which is done for God and others.

◇   ◇   ◇

Why is it that when a person learns that you have a tender heart he assumes that you also have a soft head?

◇   ◇   ◇

By lifting the burden of others we lose our own.

◇   ◇   ◇

We are interested in others when they are interested in us.

◇   ◇   ◇

No one ever solves the hurt of the world by feeling sorry for himself.

◇   ◇   ◇

Happiness adds and multiplies as we divide it with others.

◇   ◇   ◇

You can't spell *brothers* and not spell *others*.

◇ ◇ ◇

Christian people may, and do, disagree one with another, but that is no reason to be disagreeable with each other.

◇ ◇ ◇

Are you bearing one another's burdens, or bearing down on them?

◇ ◇ ◇

Forget yourself for others, and others will not forget you.

◇ ◇ ◇

A kindly deed at the right moment is worth a hundred kindly thoughts.

OURSELVES

I wish I were big enough to honestly admit all my short-comings; brilliant enough to accept flattery without its making me arrogant; tall enough to tower above deceit; strong enough to welcome criticism; compassionate enough to understand human frailties; wise enough to recognize my mistakes; humble enough to appreciate greatness; staunch enough to be thoughtful of my neighbor; and righteous enough to be devoted to the love of God.

◇ ◇ ◇

So much of life's frustration, pain, and unhappiness comes because we make ourselves the centers of our lives! We insist on living motivated by a self-regard that throws life out of focus.

◇ ◇ ◇

It is always easy to believe that a proposal is just if we get the advantage of it.

◇ ◇ ◇

Take an interest in something besides yourself.

◇ ◇ ◇

The more a man knows about himself, the less he says about it.

◇ ◇ ◇

I will chide no brother in the world but myself, against whom I know most faults.

—*William Shakespeare*

◇ ◇ ◇

No one ever does us as much harm as we do to ourselves.

◇ ◇ ◇

A good many of us make the mistake of taking ourselves at our own estimate.

◇ ◇ ◇

A man wrapped up in himself makes a mighty small package.

◇ ◇ ◇

Always take your job seriously—never yourself.

◇ ◇ ◇

He that falls in love with himself will find no rival.

—*Benjamin Franklin*

OUTREACH

Unless an idea, a principle, is incarnate in a person or an act or a policy, it is without meaning.

◇ ◇ ◇

We must reach out or pass out.

◇ ◇ ◇

The world is full of needs and sorrows and weakness. People seem to scent out the man or woman who is strong or poised, who has a Source of supply that does not give out;

they are quick to come for help with their burdens and problems.

—*Bertha Munro in "Truth for Today"*

◇   ◇   ◇

Bertha Munro, writing about Dr. E. E. Angell, said, "He clung to the wayward to save them."

◇   ◇   ◇

Christians are a concerned people—concerned with the needs of their fellowmen. Dr. P. F. Bresee said it so well: "We are debtor to ALL men to give them the gospel in the same measure as we have received it."

◇   ◇   ◇

Shall I thank God for bread,
And for the safety of the place I lay my head?
In the din of crashing worlds
Shot through with screams of pain,
I will do better, far,
To thank my God that I am strong enough
To share my bread;
Alert enough to tell those blinded by their woe
That I still see a star.
When hungry children shake with fright,
What can it mean to God that I am safe at night?

—*Anonymous*

◇   ◇   ◇

Care so deeply for others that among the famished one feels actual hunger, among the shoeless one's feet sting with frostbite on a cold morning.

—*Frank Buchman*

◇   ◇   ◇

Do people sense that they matter to God because they matter to us?

—*Ernest T. Campbell*

◇   ◇   ◇

195

The principle of involvement with the need of others reaches out beyond your personal relationships, your immediate circle of friends and acquaintances. It reaches to the ends of the earth. It involves every living person.

◇   ◇   ◇

O Lord, let no selfish purpose, no stupidity, no lack of concern, no lowered standard of behavior make it harder for anyone about me this day. Give me a glad heart, a kind tongue, a radiant spirit. And help me to live with eternity's values in mind.

◇   ◇   ◇

A five-word biography of Jesus: He "went about doing good."

◇   ◇   ◇

The epitaph above George Washington Carver's grave tells the summary of his life: "He could have added fortune to fame, but caring for neither, he found happiness and honor in being helpful to the world."

◇   ◇   ◇

I was hungry, and you formed a humanities club and discussed my hunger.
Thank you.
I was imprisoned, and you crept off quietly to your chapel in the cellar and prayed for my release.
I was naked, and in your mind you debated the morality of my appearance.
I was sick, and you knelt and thanked God for your health.
I was homeless, and you preached to me of the spiritual shelter of the love of God.
I was lonely, and you left me alone to pray for me.
You seem so holy, so close to God, but I'm still very hungry and lonely and cold.

—*"Christianity Today"*

◇   ◇   ◇

196

How dry, how parched as a desert, is the world around us! Men and women dying of spiritual thirst! "He that believeth on me, as the scripture hath said, out of his . . . [inward parts] shall flow rivers of living water."

◇ ◇ ◇

God, let me be aware.
Stab my soul fiercely awake with others' pain.
Let me walk seeing horror and stain.
Let my hands, groping, find other hands.
Give me the heart that divines, understands.
Give me courage, wounded, to fight.
Flood me with knowledge, drench me in light.
Please, keep me eager just to do my share,
God—let me be aware.
                                    —*Miriam Teichner*

◇ ◇ ◇

God forbid that we who name the name of Christ should fail to embrace the needy of earth in our kinship, our love, our responsibility.

◇ ◇ ◇

On a memorial tablet in Oxford erected to Lewis Nettleship, there are these words, "He loved great things and thought little of himself; desiring neither fame nor influence, he won the devotion of men and was a power in their lives."

◇ ◇ ◇

Self exists to be abdicated. In self-giving we touch a rhythm, not only of all creation, but of all being, for the Eternal Word also gives himself in sacrifice.
                                    —*C. S. Lewis*

◇ ◇ ◇

God-centeredness versus self-objectification.

◇ ◇ ◇

When God's redemption becomes operative in a life, it will rush through to other lives. It is a dynamic, creative, living power which cannot be confined, contained or corralled, compromised or corrupted.

◇ ◇ ◇

He cannot heal who has not suffered much,
For only sorrow, sorrow understands.
They will not come for healing at our touch
Who have not seen the scars on our hands.

—*Edwin Poteet*

◇ ◇ ◇

Who is so low that I am not his brother?
Who is so high that I've no path to him?
Who is so poor I may not feel his hunger?
Who is so rich I may not pity him?
May none, then, call on me for understanding;
May none, then, turn to me for help in pain,
And drain alone his bitter cup of sorrow,
Or find he knocks upon my heart in vain.

—*S. Ralph Harlow*

◇ ◇ ◇

If there is a contemporary word which expresses the heart of Wesleyanism or, more familiarly, holiness, it is *involvement*. How we draw back from involvement! Involvement is holiness expressing itself in love.

◇ ◇ ◇

As ambassadors, what is our message that we are commissioned to give? The gospel. Don't argue it; don't discuss it as you would politics. Proclaim it. Witness to it. How desperately the world needs that message of reconciliation! Will you let your world hear it? Your home, your neighborhood, your business, your social circle?

◇ ◇ ◇

Jesus condemned halfheartedness toward God and hard-heartedness toward men.

◇   ◇   ◇

The Church is not sufficiently involved in the heartache of modern society.

—*Andrew W. Blackwood, Jr.*

◇   ◇   ◇

There is nothing but hypocrisy in a holiness that is without compassion, concern, and deep caring.

◇   ◇   ◇

People must have priority in our lives. Homes are made of people. Neighbors are people; children are people; and even salesmen are people. The ones we rub elbows with, the hurrying crowd, are people.

◇   ◇   ◇

There is a destiny that makes us brothers;
  None goes his way alone.
All that we send into the lives of others
  Comes back into our own.

—*Edwin Markham*

◇   ◇   ◇

Go! The world's need is so desperate, the plan of salvation so complete, the Christian experience so transforming, the resources of God so adequate!

◇   ◇   ◇

The Christian religion begins in passive voice—receiving; then having freely received, openhandedly, joyously gives.

◇   ◇   ◇

You are writing each day a letter to men;
  Take care that the writing is true.
'Tis the only gospel that some men will read—
  That gospel according to you.

◇   ◇   ◇

199

The proof of our faith is in the touch of our lives. Every day we touch people with our lives. What happens? When Christ touched people, something happened.

◇　◇　◇

Everyone has something to give out of his inner life and character.

—*Robert A. Williams*

◇　◇　◇

No man is ever completely worthless. He can always serve as a horrible example.

◇　◇　◇

To make Him real to others He must first be real to you.

◇　◇　◇

God wants us to be like Jesus, who came into the world to save the world. And this demands an attitude of both separation from the world in its sin and identification with the world in its need. Without separation—the difference Christ makes—we have an audience but nothing to say. Without identification, we have something to say but no audience.

—*Leighton Ford*

◇　◇　◇

You can never give another person what you have found in Christ: peace, joy, satisfaction. But you can make him hungry for what you have.

◇　◇　◇

Call no man worthless for whom Christ died.

◇　◇　◇

A church that is not reaching out is passing out.

PARENTS/FAMILY

Churchgoing families are happier families.

◇　◇　◇

The family that prays together stays together.

◇   ◇   ◇

A successful parent studies the art of speaking in the spirit of love, by striving to make his whole life an attractive example of what he has taught.

—*Andrew Murray*

◇   ◇   ◇

God made us a family. We need one another; we love one another. We forgive one another. We work together; we play together; we worship together. Together we use God's Word; together we grow in Christ. Together we love all men; together we serve our God. Together we hope for heaven, through Christ, our Lord. These are our hopes and ideals. Help us attain them, O God!

◇   ◇   ◇

A young bride was dismayed when she remembered that she had forgotten to put baking powder in the cake she had just put in the oven. Her husband suggested adding it at the present stage of the proceedings, but his bride reminded him that some things are put in at the start or you don't get them in at all. How true this is of children! No amount of teaching and underscoring in later years can make up for a lack of early Christian nurture.

◇   ◇   ◇

No better advice for parents has ever been given than that offered by Moses: "Thou shalt teach them diligently unto thy children, and shalt talk of them when thou sittest in thine house." The idea was to make the law of God penetrate deeply into the minds and hearts of the growing generation.

◇   ◇   ◇

The electric razor took away the razor strop; furnaces took away the woodshed; tax worries took away the hair and the hairbrush. No wonder kids are running wild these days. Dad ran out of weapons.

◇   ◇   ◇

A child matures by testing himself against limits set by loving adults.

◇   ◇   ◇

"Listen" ought to be tattooed over every parent's heart.

◇   ◇   ◇

What are young people saying in trying to communicate with their parents?

Love Me! I need you!

Respect me. I am an individual.

Trust me—I must learn to make my own decisions.

Accept me, even though at the moment you can't agree with my ideas.

Forgive me—and then let's forget it.

Be honest with me. Tell it like it is.

Listen to me—maybe I have a good idea.

Teach me of Christ—by your everyday life!

—*Elizabeth C. Jackson*

◇   ◇   ◇

Any kid who has two parents who are interested in him, and a houseful of books, isn't poor.

—*Sam Levenson*

◇   ◇   ◇

When the voice and language of authority are the same as the voice and language of love, then obedience and all other forms of agreeable and acceptable behavior are easier for a child. Telling a child we love him is many things besides pet names and endearments, though they are eloquent too. It's praise for accomplishment. It's permission to try and encouragement to try again. It's acceptance of slow progress, lack of blame for failure. It's a jubilant hug, an unexpected smile. It's rules and warnings given to save

202

hurts and frights. It's a cared-for bump, a comforted fear, a surprise, a treat, a good-night story, a light left on in the hall. It's patience while a child learns the ways of a grown-up world.

—*Stanley L. Harrison, M.D., in "American Academy of Pediatrics"*

◇　◇　◇

If you are a happy parent, you give your son or daughter an invaluable legacy. It doesn't matter too much whether you are rich or poor; if the choice is between happy poor and unhappy rich the children of a laughing pauper are the ones to envy. For they will grow up with the expectation that life is good, that the world is a sunny and friendly place, that other people are as human and decent as they are, that it is fun to be alive. And with that attitude, they can accomplish almost anything.

—*Guy Wright in "San Francisco Examiner"*

◇　◇　◇

As you mother them, don't smother them.

PATIENCE
A diamond is a piece of coal that stuck to the job.

◇　◇　◇

Patience and diligence, like faith, move mountains.

◇　◇　◇

Patience is bitter, but its fruit is sweet.

◇　◇　◇

The feet that wait for God are soonest at the goal.

PEACE
Where to find spiritual security? In the intervals of serenity; in the satisfactions of the spirit; in the foundations of

right living; in the resources of divine love; in the risks of unselfishness.

◇ ◇ ◇

A committed life can do so much for us—give us serenity and tranquility in a mad, bewildered, feverish world.

◇ ◇ ◇

An unfaltering trust in God will give us an inner calm regardless of the storm raging around us. It will give us peace in a troubled world torn by strife and hatred, and "man's inhumanity to man."

◇ ◇ ◇

Distractions must be conquered or they will conquer us. So let us cultivate simplicity; let us want fewer things; let us walk in the Spirit; let us fill our minds with the Word of God and our hearts with praise. In that way we can live in peace even in such a distraught world as this.

—*"Alliance Weekly"*

◇ ◇ ◇

Deep within us all there is an amazing inner sanctuary of the soul, a holy place, a Divine Center, a speaking Voice, to which we may continuously return.

PEACEMAKING

Most of us are all for the peacemakers until they go to tinkering with our favorite tariff law.

◇ ◇ ◇

Never pick a quarrel, even when it's ripe.

PERSEVERANCE

People who succeed are like postage stamps. They stick till they get there.

◇ ◇ ◇

A quitter never wins, and a winner never quits.

◇   ◇   ◇

When you take your stand for righteousness, remain standing!

◇   ◇   ◇

Looking ahead is a good way to keep from falling behind.

◇   ◇   ◇

Things turn up for the man who digs.

◇   ◇   ◇

Good starters and good stayers are not necessarily the same people.

◇   ◇   ◇

Keep on doing what it took to get started.

◇   ◇   ◇

If you are headed in the right direction, you make progress as long as you keep moving.

◇   ◇   ◇

The one thing worse than a quitter is the man who is afraid to begin.

◇   ◇   ◇

There is hope for the man who keeps pressing on.

PESSIMISM

A pessimist is a person who is seasick during the entire voyage of life.

◇   ◇   ◇

You might as well not eat supper, because you'll just be hungry again by bedtime, anyway.

◇   ◇   ◇

The reason most committees are made up of pessimists is that the optimists were too busy to come.

PLEASURES

Seek no pleasure that omits God.

◇ ◇ ◇

The greatest play is your work.

◇ ◇ ◇

Is your work a pleasure? Your job takes up about one-third of your life, captivates a portion of your mind long after you have punched the time clock, sometimes steals your sleep, and may even creep into your dreams. Don't count minutes to closing time! Determine to enjoy your daily routine! It's not just a way to make a living—it's your life!

◇ ◇ ◇

A good time is a pleasure which has no aftermath of regret.

◇ ◇ ◇

Don't let recreation become wreck-reation.

POSSESSIONS

When an affluent society would coax us to believe that happiness consists in the size of our automobiles, the impressiveness of our houses, and the expensiveness of our clothes, Jesus reminds us, "A man's life consisteth not in the abundance of the things which he possesseth."

—*Martin Luther King*

◇ ◇ ◇

I will set no value on anything I have or may possess except in relation to the kingdom of God.

—*David Livingstone*

◇ ◇ ◇

Julian Huxley reminds us that the hearts of modern men, whose lives are full of glitter and gadgets, have a blank where God should be.

◇ ◇ ◇

Most of us would be satisfied with just a little, just enough to make our neighbors envious.

◇ ◇ ◇

Riches either serve or govern the possessor.

◇ ◇ ◇

Tenderly, carefully I carried bone china teacups to the mission field. A few months later they were shattered with one sickening blow, but by then I was accustomed to sharing the tin cans of my African neighbors, and hardly noticed.

◇ ◇ ◇

Do good with what thou hast, or it will do thee no good.

—*William Penn*

◇ ◇ ◇

What you are counts for more than what you have.

◇ ◇ ◇

He who has God has all.

◇ ◇ ◇

We do not own what our hands can grasp, but what our hearts can compass.

◇ ◇ ◇

Learn to hold loosely all that is not eternal.

POWER

We limit God and keep His power from working through us by settling down into a state of spiritual mediocrity, neither very good nor very bad. Commonplace. Ordinary.

◇ ◇ ◇

Seven blocks to spiritual power and progress:
1. Materiality
2. Pressure of conformity
3. The price

4. Distorted concept of faith and what constitutes spirituality
5. Poor sense of loyalty
6. Lack of obedience
7. Neglect of inner resources

—Roy Burkhart

◇   ◇   ◇

Through self-discipline and by the leadings of the Holy Spirit we tap vast resources of moral and spiritual power.

◇   ◇   ◇

Ideas are the most powerful things in the world.

◇   ◇   ◇

Every one of us has untapped resources of power.

◇   ◇   ◇

Steam is power caught in the cylinder if it does not escape through the whistle.

◇   ◇   ◇

There is a healing something at work in the world; and when you and I have blundered about and come to the end of our resources, there are open to us great reservoirs of power which we can't begin to tap until we've despaired of our own.

◇   ◇   ◇

It is always easier to set up machinery than it is to generate power.

◇   ◇   ◇

Power is not shown by striking hard or often, but by striking true.

PRAISE

The fellow who sings his own praise is seldom asked for an encore.

◇   ◇   ◇

It is always easy to enjoy the man who compliments us.

◇ ◇ ◇

You seldom make a father feel bad by speaking well of his children.

◇ ◇ ◇

Big people give praise; little people seek it.

◇ ◇ ◇

Praise loudly; blame softly.

◇ ◇ ◇

Praise either mellows one's heart or swells one's head.

◇ ◇ ◇

The attitude of praise is characteristic of a Christian.

◇ ◇ ◇

To give praise is more blessed than to receive it.

PRAYER

In prayer we receive strength to offset lassitude, indifference, apathy, absorption with the world.

◇ ◇ ◇

Cultivation of the inner life requires withdrawal, solitude, quiet moments of being alone with God in prayer and communion.

◇ ◇ ◇

Prayer does not consist in battering the walls of heaven for personal benefits or the success of our plans; rather it is the committing of ourselves for the carrying out of His purposes.

◇ ◇ ◇

The fewer the words, the better prayer.

—*Martin Luther*

◇ ◇ ◇

Failure in prayer is due to feebleness of faith and want of intensity in desire. The result is lackluster lives, dullness of soul, and heaviness of spirit.

◇ ◇ ◇

Prayer calls for self-discipline. When you feel most disinclined to pray, yield not to it, but strive and endeavor to pray even when you feel that you cannot pray.

◇ ◇ ◇

If you are asking me about getting alone and spending long periods of time on my knees, then I would have to say that I am relatively a prayerless man. But if you accept praying without ceasing as a continual, humble communion with God, day and night, under all circumstances, the pouring out of my heart to God in continual, unbroken fellowship—then I can say that I pray without ceasing.

—Max Reich, as told by A. W. Tozer

◇ ◇ ◇

Faith that God will answer prayer is based on three things:
1. Faith in God as a Rewarder of them that diligently seek Him; unwavering trust and confidence.
2. Harmony of our request with His will.
3. God's freedom in use of ways and means; submission to Him.

◇ ◇ ◇

There is the art of prayer, learned by practice, by doing; it is the opposite of theory. And there is the spontaneity of prayer: "Lord, save us, or we perish!" In emergencies man instinctively turns to God.

◇ ◇ ◇

Through prayer cultivate the habit of "no limitation." Nothing too small; nothing too big; no area of life where God is shut out.

◇ ◇ ◇

One's actions, one's belief, one's prayer, one's work must all be of a piece.

◇   ◇   ◇

I pray not for wealth although I could use it; not for strength although I need it; not for wisdom although I lack it. My one wish would be that I may have grace given me to be a man to the end, and to the end love my brother man with all the passion of my soul.

—*Edward Steiner*

◇   ◇   ◇

Prayer is not to ask what we wish of God, but what He wishes of us.

◇   ◇   ◇

Prayer is not the breaking down of the reluctance of God. It is taking hold of the willingness of God.

◇   ◇   ◇

The wings of prayer carry high and far.

◇   ◇   ◇

P-raying
R-egularly
A-lways
Y-ields
E-ternal
R-ewards

◇   ◇   ◇

Prayer is a sustaining power in our daily lives.

◇   ◇   ◇

Prayer is the native and deepest impulse of the soul of man.

—*Thomas Carlyle*

◇   ◇   ◇

Daily prayers are the best remedy for daily cares.

◇   ◇   ◇

Prayer without work is hypocrisy; work without prayer is presumption.

◇   ◇   ◇

When in doubt, pray.

◇   ◇   ◇

Take time to pray—it helps reveal God and cleanses the dust from your eyes.

◇   ◇   ◇

A little talk with Jesus—how it smooths the rugged road!

◇   ◇   ◇

Men who pray much bray little.

◇   ◇   ◇

When thou prayest, rather let thy heart be without words than thy words without heart.

◇   ◇   ◇

Somewhere, someway, sometime each day turn aside and stop and pray.

◇   ◇   ◇

Your praying will stop your sinning or your sinning will stop your praying.

◇   ◇   ◇

The Christian on his knees sees more than the philosopher on tiptoes.

◇   ◇   ◇

Prayer was never intended as a laborsaving device.

◇   ◇   ◇

It is easier to sing during an altar call than pray, but the results are far less.

◇   ◇   ◇

When thou prayest to thy Father, thou needest only thy need.

◇   ◇   ◇

Secret prayer is the fountain of all other prayer.

◇   ◇   ◇

When it is hardest to pray, it is time to pray hardest.

◇   ◇   ◇

Some pray-ers sound as if they never expect God to answer.

◇   ◇   ◇

Resolve that your prayers shall no longer be a form but a force.

◇   ◇   ◇

He stands best who kneels most.

◇   ◇   ◇

The hour of opportunity lies near the hour of prayer.

◇   ◇   ◇

Our prayer and God's mercy are like two buckets in a well: while the one ascends, the other descends.

◇   ◇   ◇

He prayeth best who loveth best.

◇   ◇   ◇

Prayer brings us what God wants us to have.

◇   ◇   ◇

We do not really pray until we are honest with ourselves as well as with God.

◇   ◇   ◇

Satan trembles when he sees
The weakest saint upon his knees.

◇   ◇   ◇

Prayer is a shield to the soul, a sacrifice to God, and a scourge for Satan.

◇   ◇   ◇

Prayer is not eloquence, but earnestness.

◇   ◇   ◇

One man prayed: "Dear Lord, don't let nothing get ahold of me that You and me can't handle!"

◇ ◇ ◇

No prayer ever produces much in the way of results which is prayed without thinking.

◇ ◇ ◇

Prayer requires more of the heart than of the tongue.

◇ ◇ ◇

Getting on your knees will help you get on your feet.

◇ ◇ ◇

Things begun in prayer usually end in power.

◇ ◇ ◇

If you are too busy to pray, you are too busy.

◇ ◇ ◇

The best prayer is the one that ends in action.

◇ ◇ ◇

Minutes spent with the Master in the morning may mean hours of blessing for the rest of the day.

◇ ◇ ◇

Prayer should be the key of the day and the lock of the night.

◇ ◇ ◇

It is hard to hate the person you are praying for.

◇ ◇ ◇

Pray big prayers and you will get big answers.

◇ ◇ ◇

Prayer is the Christian's vital breath.

◇ ◇ ◇

Prayer changes things; praise keeps what prayer has changed.

◇ ◇ ◇

Prayer drives away fear and trouble.

◇ ◇ ◇

When your knees knock, kneel on them.

PRAYERLESSNESS
Most of us are carrying an overdraft on the Bank of Heaven.

◇ ◇ ◇

Because of failure in prayer men are weak when they might be strong, anxious and full of cares when they might have peace. Some go through the forms of prayer but they do not know this life of trustful fellowship, implicit confidence in God.

◇ ◇ ◇

The one concern of Satan is to keep the saints from prayer. He fears nothing from prayerless studies, prayerless work, prayerless religion. He laughs at our toil, mocks at our wisdom, and trembles when we pray.

—*Andrew Bonar*

◇ ◇ ◇

The prevailing temper of our generation is not conducive to prayer, devotion, self-examination. With our enthusiasm for program participation, our competitive spirit even in church matters, it is easy to neglect spiritual nurture.

◇ ◇ ◇

You can do more than pray AFTER you have prayed, but you can't do more than pray UNTIL you have prayed.

◇ ◇ ◇

Seven days without prayer make one weak.

PREJUDICE
It is always so easy to believe the evidence which supports our prejudices.

◇ ◇ ◇

A prejudice knows no logic.

◇ ◇ ◇

You can't hold a man down without staying down with him.

—*Booker T. Washington*

◇ ◇ ◇

The greatest hazard toward progressive thinking is prejudice.

◇ ◇ ◇

The color problem will never be solved by those who always see red.

◇ ◇ ◇

Our dearest pets are our prejudices.

◇ ◇ ◇

Face facts and turn your back on your prejudice.

◇ ◇ ◇

The difference between a prejudice and a conviction is that you can explain a conviction without getting mad.

PRIDE

A great heart and a big head seldom go together.

◇ ◇ ◇

It is a sorry spectacle when pride takes the place of humility.

◇ ◇ ◇

More forgiving would be done if less personal pride were involved.

◇ ◇ ◇

When a lot of people begin to blow their own horns, there is sure to be some very poor music.

◇ ◇ ◇

Even a little pat on the back can make the chest stick out.

◇ ◇ ◇

Big heads offer ample room for small minds to rattle.

PROBLEMS

We worship a God who is greater than any of our problems.

◇　◇　◇

If we had no tough problems to solve, most anybody could do our job.

◇　◇　◇

We have magnified our problems until the problems have multiplied, leaving us stupefied.

◇　◇　◇

The best angle from which to approach a problem is the try-angle.

◇　◇　◇

Problems often are solved by faith after reason failed.

◇　◇　◇

We do not solve problems by running away from them.

◇　◇　◇

The Saviour can solve every problem—but sometimes He needs us to hold the flashlight.

PROFANITY

Profanity is the effort of a feeble mind trying to express itself forcibly.

◇　◇　◇

Profanity is a confession that we have a limited vocabulary.

◇　◇　◇

O thou, that dost not cuss, dost thou use bywords? *Gee,* according to Webster, is "a minced form of *Jesus,* used in mild oaths." *Gosh,* "a softened form of 'God' used as a mild oath." (*Darn* and *heck* are also "no-nos.")

217

PROGRESS
He who does not look forward remains behind.

◇ ◇ ◇

There is a difference between spiritual progress and a religious hurrah.

◇ ◇ ◇

The danger of all great institutions is that they begin to worship their own past. You cannot go back; you must either go forward or perish.

—William Barclay, quoting Harnack

◇ ◇ ◇

We can use the past for inspiration, and we can use the past for guidance; but we can seldom or never use the past as a pattern for the present.

—William Barclay

◇ ◇ ◇

He who walks with Christ gets somewhere.

◇ ◇ ◇

It is a dangerous thing to suggest new ideas in old churches.

◇ ◇ ◇

You can't push yourself forward by patting yourself on the back.

◇ ◇ ◇

The turtle makes progress only when he sticks his neck out.

PROMISES
If we have God's say-so behind us, the most amazing strength comes, and we learn to sing in the ordinary days and ways.

—Oswald Chambers

◇ ◇ ◇

218

Promises may win friends; only performances will keep them.

◇ ◇ ◇

Our capacity in spiritual matters is measured by the promises of God.

—*Oswald Chambers*

◇ ◇ ◇

A man is known by the promises he keeps.

◇ ◇ ◇

The devil makes many fair promises; but has never been known to keep one in the end.

◇ ◇ ◇

God's promises are life preservers that keep the soul from sinking in the sea of trouble.

QUITTING

Worse than a quitter is one who is afraid to begin.

RACISM

Racism is the assumption of superiority and the arrogance that goes with it.

◇ ◇ ◇

The Church, it appears, is on trial. How will it respond to social unrest? Will it proclaim—unafraid—that man is not to be viewed by the color of his skin, nor by the poverty of his existence, but by the possibilities that might be wrapped up in him as a person, waiting to be tapped for good?

—*C. Neil Strait*

◇ ◇ ◇

Dr. Charles Drew, Negro physician who discovered blood plasma, bled to death because he was not admitted to a white hospital.

READING

Reading molds our thinking and our beliefs. It contributes to our cultural standards, our moral ideals, our information, our inspiration, our spiritual growth.

—*Kathryn Johnson*

◇   ◇   ◇

Books are silent, but they speak.

—*Russell H. Conwell*

◇   ◇   ◇

By their reading tables ye shall know them.

◇   ◇   ◇

Good books give new views to life and teach us how to live.

◇   ◇   ◇

Let me read always as a Christian. Help me to scan books as I would read men, to seek the good and shun the evil. Let me not soil my mind with what is foul, nor indulge willingly in fancy what would shame me in life. Let me not be selfish, that my brain become no tower of Babel, no high tower of pride and confusion, but that through partaking of the fruitage of the toils of others I may myself be better furnished for service to mankind.

—*Kenneth J. Foreman*

◇   ◇   ◇

Reading between the lines is reading dangerously.

◇   ◇   ◇

A man is himself plus the books he reads.

—*S. Parkes Cadman*

◇   ◇   ◇

Right reading is a fountain of wisdom.

◇   ◇   ◇

The publication of a truly great book is a news event of the first magnitude.

◇   ◇   ◇

The *New York Times* discovered that 25 percent of college students have not read a book in the past year; only 17 percent of American adults at any time are reading a book, and almost half the homes have no bookcases. We are simply not devotees of the art of reading, and the disastrous result of such a delinquency is superficial thinking, which is of far deeper consequence than merely getting a better job. An impoverished mind is a tragedy. Serious reading not only plows the subsoil of the mind but stirs the fountains of the soul.

—*J. Fred Parker*

◇   ◇   ◇

Salvage the fragments of time—5 or 10 minutes—that otherwise would be wasted. Redeem the time; read!

◇   ◇   ◇

The average reader reads 300 words a minute. If you read 300 words a minute for 15 minutes a day, every day, 365 days a year, you will have read 1,642,500 words during that year, or 22 full-length books. Fifteen minutes a day means 2 books a month, more than 20 a year, or 1,000 books or more during your lifetime! Most people don't read more than 5 books a year.

◇   ◇   ◇

Your spiritual reading should in some respects be like a meditation; you should watch for God's action within you and pause when you feel your heart touched by what you read. Always read with a view to practice.

—*Jean Nicolas Grou*

◇   ◇   ◇

Not only is there a wide variety among books, but also among readers. A particular book may be pronounced "chaff" by one reader and "wheat" by another. Reading tastes differ. Also, ability to handle a little chaff with the wheat varies. There are those who can read any and all opinions on a subject and still know what they believe; others get agitated the moment they read an opinion contrary to their cherished convictions.

◇ ◇ ◇

There are four kinds of readers:

(1) Hourglass readers, whose reading runs in and out and leaves nothing.

(2) Sponge readers, who imbibe all, but only to give it out again as they got it, and perhaps not as clean.

(3) Jelly-bag readers, who keep the dregs and refuse, and let the pure run through.

(4) Diamond readers, who cast aside all that is worthless, and hold only the gems.

—William Coleridge

◇ ◇ ◇

It is impossible to divorce spirituality and holy living from devotional reading. As the literal flame expires without fuel, as life itself is dependent upon nourishment, so it is with the spiritual. All the processes of Christian growth are vitally connected with devotional reading. Prayer, testimony, personal work, church attendance—all fall into disuse when not stimulated and fed by devotional reading. Spiritual reading invigorates the intellect, refreshes the emotions, and through them reaches the will. And I submit that it requires a studied, planned, systematic program of inner-life religion to "maintain the spiritual glow."

REBUKE

Next time someone "bawls you out" try the soft-answer-turneth-away-wrath theory.

—Earl Riney

RELIGION

Fire does not mean rant, or noise, or ruthless self-will. It acts differently on different material and in different people, but in all it burns, kindles, and glows. It is religion at white-heat.

—*Samuel Chadwick*

◇   ◇   ◇

Between a man's inner religion and his outward life there should be no divider. The two are inseparable.

◇   ◇   ◇

In times like these we need a religion of reality, a religion that really gets us, that possesses us, that sends us, that makes us forget ourselves, our comforts, our materialistic goals and aspirations, our petty purposes, our shortsighted plans.

◇   ◇   ◇

The test of our religion is how we live because of what we believe.

◇   ◇   ◇

To what extent does my religion affect my life? What does it do for me, outwardly, inwardly? What changes, transformations in attitudes, habits, personality have been wrought?

◇   ◇   ◇

When we speak of real religion we mean a faith, a power, a supernatural incentive which makes itself felt in every circumstance of life.

◇   ◇   ◇

Real religion finds expression in that to which we give our interest, our enthusiasm, and our devotion.

◇   ◇   ◇

Many professed Christians have the sort of compartmentalized religion Margarie Kinnan Rawlings speaks of in *Cross Creek*. She tells of a Florida "cracker"—dirty,

ragged, lazy, profane, and illegal fisherman and moon-
shiner, "borrower" of loose property. When asked to go
fishing on Sunday, he said, "No, I can't do that; I wa'n't
raised up that-a-way."

◇ ◇ ◇

Real religion integrates, brings together disparate parts
into a harmonious whole; gives balance, symmetry. No
more conflicting desires, crosscurrents of purpose, double-
mindedness.

◇ ◇ ◇

Real religion is timeless. It gives forgiveness for the past;
sins forgotten, soul restored, faculties redeemed. It gives
present victory with serenity, guidance, growth. It brings
hope, expectancy, anticipation for the future.

◇ ◇ ◇

Real religion means life and power and beauty and harmony for daily living in this materialistic, complex,
pleasure-oriented, bewildering, tragedy-filled world; helps
us to live gloriously.

◇ ◇ ◇

It is possible to be inoculated so often with the dead germs
of religion that one becomes immune to the real thing.

—*Sam Shoemaker*

◇ ◇ ◇

Religion cultivates the inward, outward, upward look.

◇ ◇ ◇

Real religion is more than formal ritual, more than a cold
creed. It has a creed, but it centers in personal experience.
Real religion has at least three elements: heart satisfaction (a personal seeking and finding of God); worship (a
personal adoring of God); consecration (a personal giving
of self to God).

—*Bertha Munro*

◇ ◇ ◇

224

Vital religion is not based on doctrine, not on church affiliation, but on spiritual forces which can transform, illumine, direct, and empower life.

◇   ◇   ◇

If our religion is real, it will affect all our relationships—friends, family, enemies, the underprivileged, peoples of other races.

◇   ◇   ◇

Legitimate business never conflicts with true religion.

◇   ◇   ◇

Religious externals may have a meaning for the God-inhabited soul; for any others they are not only useless but may actually become snares, deceiving them into a false and perilous sense of security.

—*A. W. Tozer*

◇   ◇   ◇

In summer religion is sometimes snowed under.

◇   ◇   ◇

Monday behavior is the acid test of your religion.

◇   ◇   ◇

Religion is not much use until it gets into the heart.

◇   ◇   ◇

We live not that we may be religious, but we are religious that we may live.

◇   ◇   ◇

The deadliest Pharisaism today is not hypocrisy, but unconscious unreality.

—*Oswald Chambers*

◇   ◇   ◇

Men trained in intellect but not in religion and morals will become a menace to the country.

—*Theodore Roosevelt*

◇   ◇   ◇

That religion that makes you want to fight your brother never came from your Father.

◇ ◇ ◇

The man who is ashamed of his religion has a religion he ought to be ashamed of.

◇ ◇ ◇

An easygoing religion makes the going easy for the evil.

◇ ◇ ◇

Religion and common sense are born twins.

◇ ◇ ◇

An upright man can never be a downright failure.

◇ ◇ ◇

Any doctrine that makes a man quarrelsome is poor religion.

◇ ◇ ◇

A man's religion is measured by his everyday conduct.

◇ ◇ ◇

Religion is meant to be bread for daily use, not cake for special occasions.

◇ ◇ ◇

Religion, like medicine, has to be taken to bring results.

◇ ◇ ◇

Don't use religion as a spare tire—only in emergencies.

◇ ◇ ◇

Easygoing religion makes weak souls.

◇ ◇ ◇

Religion in the past tense becomes pretense.

REPENTANCE

Penitence is an attitude of mind to which a man must be reawakened every day.

—*William Barclay*

◇ ◇ ◇

Too many of us hope and work in a vague sort of way for a better world without first coming to terms with ourselves. And yet what is most deeply wrong with the world is often but a reflection of what is most inwardly wrong with each of us.

◇　◇　◇

Intellectual belief produces no spiritual experience. Belief in Jesus Christ not preceded by genuine repentance and forsaking of sin leaves the heart cold and empty.

◇　◇　◇

Justice doles out the punishment that wrongdoing deserves. Mercy forgives, forgets, and restores.

◇　◇　◇

It does not take a long prayer to express penitence.

◇　◇　◇

A restored soul is better than a shot in the arm.

◇　◇　◇

Repentance was once defined by a small girl: "It's being sorry enough to quit."

◇　◇　◇

True repentance is to cease from sin.

RESPONSIBILITY

Some people grow under responsibility; others swell.

◇　◇　◇

Every Christian is responsible for adding to the defenses of justice.

RETIREMENT

> *Rest is not quitting*
> *A busy career;*
> *Rest is the fitting*
> *Of self to one's sphere.*

REVENGE

To forget wrong is the best revenge.

REVIVAL

The great evangelical revival began, not with the reclamation of the depraved, but with the enrichment of the redeemed.

—*John Henry Jowett*

REWARD

God's bookkeeper makes no mistakes.

◇　◇　◇

God rewards our fidelity.

◇　◇　◇

The reward is *in* keeping the commandments, not *for* keeping them.

◇　◇　◇

A man's reward is not only what he gets, but what he becomes.

RIGHTS

A Christian sees other people's rights as clearly as his own.

◇　◇　◇

Most of us are wasting rights which other men have fought for.

RUIN

The road to ruin is always kept in good repair, and the travelers pay the expense on it.

228

RUMORS

Did you ever hear of an idle rumor remaining idle very long?

◇ ◇ ◇

Some people are like blotters; they soak up everything but get it all backwards.

◇ ◇ ◇

Great commotions out of little rumors grow.

◇ ◇ ◇

Many people have a sense of rumor.

SACRIFICE

Harder than to leave family and friends in all-out ventures of faith is to live among them but not by their standards, walking life's ordinary paths but seeing God, mingling with the crowd but obeying higher standards, even to the point of subjecting yourself to their disapproval. That isn't easy, but who said the Christian life was easy? Jesus warned those who would follow Him that it meant hardship, leaving loved ones, forsaking home, livelihood, all that any normal person would hold dear.

SAINTS

The only instance of praying to saints mentioned in the Bible is that of the rich man in torment calling upon Abraham; and let it be remembered that it was practiced by a lost soul without success.

—Cecil

◇ ◇ ◇

No saint ever became saintly by accident.

◇ ◇ ◇

229

With the Christian faith a new power has been born into the world, which transforms men's lives and produces the highest qualities of saintliness the world has ever seen, often out of the most unpromising material.

—*Daniel Jenkins*

SALVATION/REDEMPTION

Salvation is easy because it cost God so much, but the manifestation of it in my life is difficult.

—*Oswald Chambers*

◇　◇　◇

"You are not your own." You are God's by creation and by redemption.

◇　◇　◇

Salvation comes, not by refining of base desires and by attaining lofty ideals, but by transforming power, making new creations out of old, replacing hatred with love, sin with righteousness, death with life.

◇　◇　◇

The day you turn your face from sin to God; the day you look away from your own works, your own feelings, even your own faith—unto Jesus; the day you cease struggling; the day you see that faith is simply depending upon Jesus as a bankrupt debtor depends upon his endorser; the day you begin to so depend upon and confess Christ as your Saviour; that day God will save your soul, and through that selfsame, simple faith will you become a son of God.

◇　◇　◇

Men are willing to pay a high price for damnation when salvation is free.

◇　◇　◇

Salvation makes the poorest rich.

◇　◇　◇

230

The door of salvation is always open, but God never drives anyone through it.

◇ ◇ ◇

Salvation is free because Somebody (Jesus) paid for it.

◇ ◇ ◇

Dr. Richard Niebuhr has well expressed the watered-down concept of God and of salvation which characterizes much present-day religion: "A God without wrath, calling a man without sin, to a kingdom without judgment, through a Christ without a Cross."

◇ ◇ ◇

Sin is not primarily wrongdoing; it is wrong being, deliberate independence of God.

◇ ◇ ◇

Salvation is not a spectator thing. It has no meaning, no reality, no effectiveness for you unless you participate.

◇ ◇ ◇

It is comparatively easy to make Christ the Center of our outward forms of worship or to make Him the Center of our discussions and arguments. Only a born-again experience of conversion enables one to make Him the actual governing Center of our total lives.

◇ ◇ ◇

It is only when a person has a personal encounter with God, beginning a definite relationship, that transformation takes place.

◇ ◇ ◇

It is alarmingly regrettable that many fine, respectable, wonderful people, though religious, have never entered into conscious relationship with God.

◇ ◇ ◇

"So great salvation"
    Individuality—Universality

231

Uttermost extent—Spirit, soul, body
Miracle—Transforming

◇　◇　◇

The Christian faith is basically a call to change—
> A different way to think about ourselves: Steward-
> ship.
> A different reaction to events: Commitment.
> A different way to relate to customs and ways of the
> world: Separation.

◇　◇　◇

Conversion, while it is a definite break with the past, does not immunize against the present. It is no panacea for man's difficulties. The waters will swell at his feet. The difference does not rest in a change of circumstances, but in the potential to face them. The godly person is not saved out of the world but in it.

◇　◇　◇

Man is a trinity—body, soul, and spirit. Man was originally holy but by sin he fell. The spirit became dead in sin, the soul became possessed by sin, the seed of death entered the body. By justification and regeneration man is saved; that is, the spirit is made alive. By sanctification man is saved; that is, the soul is cleansed from the inbeing of sin. By glorification man is saved; that is, the body is delivered from the seed of death and made incorruptible. Thus a full-salvation man is saved body, soul, and spirit; saved in ever point where sin affected him.

◇　◇　◇

"The Son of man is come to seek and to save." This is God's redemption. Pity those who think and teach that He came for any other purpose.

◇　◇　◇

There is much talk about peace, social conditions, race prejudice, Communism, crime, without emphasis on the

232

source; and an equal lack of guidance on how all this can be remedied—through redemption.

◇   ◇   ◇

We tend to want to merit salvation by our works. There is nothing of this miracle of redemption in our efforts, our struggles, to attain salvation.

SATAN
If Satan can use you to do some of his work, it will be more effective than if he did it himself.

SECOND COMING
The second coming of Christ is mentioned 318 times in the 210 chapters of the New Testament.

◇   ◇   ◇

I want to live as though Jesus died for me yesterday, rose this morning, and is coming again tomorrow.

◇   ◇   ◇

"In such an hour as ye think not." Failure to look daily for His appearing is conducive to complacency, the stultifying of devotion, watering down of praise, and the tendency to surround oneself with secular things—props that will go down in a moment.

◇   ◇   ◇

Look for His appearing. Never say with the scoffers, "Where is the promise of his coming?" We should live in an attitude of immediacy—the Lord may come today.

◇   ◇   ◇

Hope is indeed the "anchor of the soul"; it enables us to live each day with Christ filling our horizons.

SECRETS

If you want another to keep your secret, first keep it yourself.

SELF-CONTROL

It takes more self-control to use leisure well than workdays.

SELF-DENIAL

Self-denial is a kind of holy association with God.

SELF-PITY

Time spent in pitying oneself is the worst kind of idleness.

◇   ◇   ◇

When it comes to coddling imaginary wrongs, the average person is a faithful nurse.

SELFISHNESS

Don't conduct your life on the cafeteria style—self-service only.

◇   ◇   ◇

A man wrapped up in himself makes a small parcel.

◇   ◇   ◇

It is not God who punishes self-centeredness. It is the starved and miserable self that does its own punishing.

◇   ◇   ◇

We have a right to do as we please only when we please to do right.

◇   ◇   ◇

A self-centered person will find himself alone.

234

SEPARATION

What has become of the doctrine of separation? If believers were filled with the Spirit, would they haunt the world's gaudy fountains and brackish springs? It is mockery to profess fullness, and go about panting with thirst and gasping with vanity.

—*Samuel Chadwick*

◇　◇　◇

Stop saying Amen to what the world says and keep your soul alive.

—*Robert Louis Stevenson*

◇　◇　◇

It is not possible for men and women whose lives are given to God's way to accept the patterns of politics and economics and international relations and common social practice in our time.

◇　◇　◇

You know the truth—let your life show it.

◇　◇　◇

Sign in a church vestibule: "If you were on trial for being a Christian, would there be enough evidence to convict you?"

◇　◇　◇

If we are going to retain personal contact with the Lord Jesus Christ, it will mean there are some things we must scorn to do or to think, some legitimate things we must scorn to touch.

—*Oswald Chambers*

SERMONS

Sermonettes are just fine for Christianettes.

◇　◇　◇

Most people enjoy the sermon that someone else ought to hear.

◇ ◇ ◇

A sermon is not a failure just because it does not bear fruit within the next seven days.

◇ ◇ ◇

You can help improve your preacher's preaching by being a better hearer.

◇ ◇ ◇

It really makes very little difference who is in the pulpit if the people hear the voice of God.

◇ ◇ ◇

The best compliment that you can pay your pastor is to bring someone to hear him who has not been coming.

◇ ◇ ◇

The most embarrassing sermon a preacher could ever hear would be a record of one of his own.

◇ ◇ ◇

A sermon that is keen enough to cut into your conscience can't be called dull.

◇ ◇ ◇

I have preached to some people in times past who thought I was a fine preacher so long as I did not hit them but shot the other fellow.

◇ ◇ ◇

God can't do any more for us than we are willing to have done.

◇ ◇ ◇

There is no room for pessimism in any Christian sermon.

◇ ◇ ◇

Good sermons come from preachers who are well prayed for.

◇ ◇ ◇

When a speech falls dead on the platform, often the trouble is with its heart.

◇ ◇ ◇

The average sermon today is not calculated to put people under conviction.

◇ ◇ ◇

After a lapse of a year many an address could be delivered a second time with nobody any the wiser. This is true also the first time.

SERVICE

God's call is not to conscripts, but to volunteers.

◇ ◇ ◇

It is only the selfless me that God can use.

—*Mary Bethune*

◇ ◇ ◇

Teach us, good Lord, to serve Thee, as thou deservest:
To give and not to count the cost;
To fight and not to heed the wounds;
To toil and not to seek for rest;
To labor and not ask for any reward
Save that of knowing that we do Thy will.

—*St. Ignatius of Loyola*

◇ ◇ ◇

Christian faith leads to happiness, joy. But the road thereto sometimes is a detour. It leads through someone's hurt that you have healed; someone's faith you have firmed; someone's trust you have restored; someone's vision you have cleared; someone's burden you have shared; someone's reputation you have vindicated; someone's soul you have led to the foot of the Cross.

◇ ◇ ◇

Sensitivity to human needs and to God's guidance will lead us to some service of love.

◇ ◇ ◇

He who would be perfectly free, let him be the slave of Christ and the servant of men.

◇ ◇ ◇

Asked how he was able to overcome the barriers between the status of a professional white doctor and the Indian, Dr. Douglas Powers, who worked among the Apache Indians in the southwestern United States, said: "As a Christian doctor I consider myself a servant. You can't say much to offend a servant."

◇ ◇ ◇

Earth is filled with burning bushes of revelation, of calls to service, but only he who has his soul tuned in hears the voice of God, takes off his shoes, and worships.

◇ ◇ ◇

Be a go-getter, not a have-it-broughter.

◇ ◇ ◇

God employs no hirelings; His work is done by His sons.

◇ ◇ ◇

We are responsible for what service God is able to do through us.

◇ ◇ ◇

There is no limit as to what God can do through you if you don't care who gets the credit.

◇ ◇ ◇

Love never asks: "How much MUST I do?" But, "How much CAN I do?"

◇ ◇ ◇

"Service is LOVE made visible."

◇ ◇ ◇

"There is no substitute for consecrated shoe leather."

◇   ◇   ◇

God has given every one of us something to do in this world of His. Do we appreciate the honor enough to do it?

◇   ◇   ◇

Real joy comes not from ease or riches or from the praise of men, but from doing something worthwhile.

—Wilfred Grenfell

◇   ◇   ◇

God loves a cheerful doer, as well as a cheerful giver.

◇   ◇   ◇

Pray for a good harvest, but keep on hoeing.

◇   ◇   ◇

The vocation of every man and woman is to serve other people.

◇   ◇   ◇

To stay youthful, stay useful.

◇   ◇   ◇

God never expects any more from any man than his best.

◇   ◇   ◇

One seldom needs to travel far to find someone in need.

◇   ◇   ◇

No man can serve God by proxy.

SILENCE

I find it impossible to avoid offending guilty men, for there is no way of avoiding it but by our silence or their patience; and silent we cannot be because of God's command, and patient they cannot be because of their guilt.

—Martin Luther

◇   ◇   ◇

It often shows a fine command of language to refrain from using it.

◇　◇　◇

Stand up to be seen; speak up to be heard; shut up to be appreciated.

◇　◇　◇

There is no diplomacy like silence.

◇　◇　◇

The silent man is often worth listening to.

◇　◇　◇

Silence can't be misquoted.

◇　◇　◇

Never speak unless you can improve on silence.

◇　◇　◇

One good thing about silence is that it can't be repeated.

SIN

Separation from God is always the dreary ending of sin's sorrowful chapter.

◇　◇　◇

The penalty of sin is that gradually you get used to it and do not know that it is sin.

—*Oswald Chambers*

◇　◇　◇

We avoid facing up to sin. We avoid it by our efforts to keep the letter of the law, maintaining the mechanics of religion.

◇　◇　◇

I could not live in peace if I put the shadow of willful sin between myself and God.

—*George Eliot*

◇　◇　◇

Sin is my claim to my right to myself.
—Oswald Chambers

◇　◇　◇

No one ever trifled with sin without suffering tragic consequences.

◇　◇　◇

Sin is man's willful effort to organize his universe of values around himself as the center. Sin is self-assertion. Sin is stifling self-centeredness.

◇　◇　◇

Jesus taught that to be selfish or hard or unforgiving toward your brother is sin. To fear anything more than you fear God is sin. To love anything more than you love God is sin. To care for anything more than for the right is sin. Fear, worry, selfishness, greed, halfheartedness toward God and hardheartedness toward men—these are the sins that concerned Jesus.

◇　◇　◇

The heart of sin. Our ideas of sin may become conventional and shallow. There are those who are narrow, selfish, censorious, domineering, and yet who consider themselves unusually pious, perhaps because they observe this form or avoid that amusement. There were men in Jesus' time who ignored pride and hardness of heart but who were horrified at the breaking of some man-made Sabbath rule.

◇　◇　◇

Every sin committed began as a thought. It progresses like this: thought, act, habit, destiny.

◇　◇　◇

The whole idea of redemption is to save man from the power of sin.

◇　◇　◇

The message of God's Word is "You can be made free from sin."

◇   ◇   ◇

In our mental outlook we have to reconcile ourselves to the fact of sin as the only explanation as to why Jesus Christ came, and as the explanation of the grief and sorrow in life.

—*Oswald Chambers*

◇   ◇   ◇

Sin is a fact, not a defect; sin is red-handed mutiny against God. Either God or sin must die in my life.

—*Oswald Chambers*

◇   ◇   ◇

When will men wake up to a sense of sin in regard to the evils Jesus condemned, such as unkindness, spiritual pride, the unforgiving spirit, gossip, failure to do our duty to those who pay us to do it?

◇   ◇   ◇

Forgiveness is unreal because, in the main, the sense of sin is weak.

◇   ◇   ◇

Sin needn't be monstrous, shocking, headlining. It can be quiet, subtle, hidden, unsuspected, but its deadly erosion goes on unseen.

◇   ◇   ◇

We must never take lightly the sins of the flesh, the sins of passion. They not only destroy body and soul, but leave deep scars even when forgiveness is found and the prodigal comes home.

—*W. T. Purkiser*

◇   ◇   ◇

The gospel provides a remedy for sin. The remedy is greater than the disease. There is forgiveness for the sins of the flesh, and cleansing from the sin of the spirit.

—*W. T. Purkiser*

◇ ◇ ◇

A veneer of civilization or refinement cannot hide sin's ugliness, cruelty, deadliness, loathsomeness.

◇ ◇ ◇

Because of sin—
Man has taken the deity out of religion,
   —the supernatural out of Christianity
   —the authority from the Bible
   —God out of education
   —Morality and virtue out of literature
   —Beauty and truth out of art
   —Ethics out of business
   —Fidelity out of marriage

◇ ◇ ◇

Man has sabotaged the Bible, humanized God, defied Christ, minimized sin, secularized religion, glorified science, glamorized sex, and liquorized society.

◇ ◇ ◇

Oh, the terrible, hollow emptiness caused by sin in the life of millions; the despair, the hopelessness, the futility when life itself becomes an empty, haunted house!

◇ ◇ ◇

Sin glamorized, popularized, rationalized, naturalized!

◇ ◇ ◇

The sin they do by two and two they must answer for one by one.

—*Rudyard Kipling*

◇ ◇ ◇

Augustine wrote a biography of sin in four words: a thought, a form, a fascination, a fall.

◇ ◇ ◇

Satan is always willing to give you an excuse to indulge in sin.

◇   ◇   ◇

The Seven Cardinal Sins of the Ancients:
1. Pride
2. Covetousness
3. Lust
4. Anger
5. Gluttony
6. Envy
7. Sloth

◇   ◇   ◇

The wages of sin are always paid exactly on time.

◇   ◇   ◇

Man is not a sinner because he commits sin; he commits sin because he is a sinner, because the root of sin is in him.

◇   ◇   ◇

Our sense of sin is in proportion to our nearness to God.

◇   ◇   ◇

You have a pretty good measure of a man's religion when you know what he thinks of sin.

◇   ◇   ◇

Sin is sin, whether innate, dormant, or full-blown violence and outbreaking transgressions.

◇   ◇   ◇

The most expensive thing in the world is SIN.

◇   ◇   ◇

The pleasures of sin are "for a season," but its wages are for eternity.

◇   ◇   ◇

Sin is the only cloud without a silver lining.

◇   ◇   ◇

You may compromise with sin but sin will never compromise with you.

◇　◇　◇

The reason that sin is so attractive is due to its deceitfulness.

◇　◇　◇

No sin is ever a virtue because it is "just a little sin."

◇　◇　◇

The wages of sin have never been reduced.

◇　◇　◇

When we minimize sin, the gospel is cheapened, the Church weakened, and sinners are forgotten.

SINCERITY

There is no substitute for sincerity.

SLANDER

To ignore insults is to insure one's peace of mind.

◇　◇　◇

You never whitewash yourself by smearing somebody else.

◇　◇　◇

Truth is generally the best vindication against slander.

—*Abraham Lincoln*

◇　◇　◇

Small men do not help themselves by tearing down big men.

◇　◇　◇

Mud thrown is ground lost.

◇　◇　◇

Don't throw mud; you might miss your mark, but you are bound to get your hands dirty.

SMILE

The smile is the universal language.

◇ ◇ ◇

Sixty-six muscles are required to produce a frown and only 16 to smile. Wear a smile and save the difference.

◇ ◇ ◇

It costs so little to smile, and the returns are so great, how can we afford not to live that happy, cheerful life that is the sign of the Christian?

◇ ◇ ◇

If you hope for pleasant things to turn up, keep the corners of your mouth that way.

◇ ◇ ◇

Wrinkles should merely show where the smiles have been.

—Mark Twain

◇ ◇ ◇

A smile will get what money cannot buy.

◇ ◇ ◇

I have heard that smiles were never rationed. Why not try a few?

◇ ◇ ◇

Learn to smile; it pays.

◇ ◇ ◇

All people smile in the same language.

SORROW

Sorrow is sometimes our most rewarding experience.

◇ ◇ ◇

Dr. Ralph Sockman said that life is a passage through a schoolroom, where we are forever learning; sorrow is a required course in that schoolroom.

◇ ◇ ◇

The best way to find comfort in your own sorrow is to be so busy giving comfort to others that you forget your own.

SPEECH

Talk less, think more.

◇　◇　◇

Think twice before you speak once.

◇　◇　◇

Most of us know how to say nothing; few of us know when.

◇　◇　◇

Speech needs to be daily seasoned with grace or else it will become salted with sarcasm.
—*Raymond M. Box*

◇　◇　◇

Before speaking consider well: why you speak, what you speak, to whom you speak, and when.

◇　◇　◇

We are never hurt by the things we do not say.

◇　◇　◇

It is a great art to be able to speak forcefully without speaking viciously.

STEWARDSHIP

Reduced to its simplest terms, stewardship is an acknowledgement of responsibility.

◇　◇　◇

Material things, even our bodies, are transitory—spirits are eternal.

◇　◇　◇

When a successful businessman passes away, the question is often asked: "What did he leave?" He left everything he had. Now he has only that which he sent ahead.

◇　◇　◇

The Christian ideal is not to live lavishly, not to hoard, but to give, to share.

◇   ◇   ◇

A Christian must remember that our genuine needs—those truly essential for high-quality living—are not very numerous. Scrambling for more material things can be a snare of the devil.

◇   ◇   ◇

Our response to the love of Christ is the foundation for giving. When the individual realizes what God has done for him, he is thankful and he reaches out in response with that which is in his heart.

STRENGTH

Three things provide strength in my spirit: the warmth of concerned friends, the entireness of my own commitment, and the presence of Christ.

◇   ◇   ◇

The Church is strong enough in doctrine to save the world but weak enough in practice to become its laughingstock.

◇   ◇   ◇

Nothing is so strong as gentleness; nothing is so gentle as real strength.

—*St. Francis de Sales*

STUBBORNNESS

Says the stubborn soul: "My mind is made up. Don't confuse me with the facts."

SUCCESS

Don't be discouraged by failure or satisfied with success.

◇   ◇   ◇

Successful living is pretty much getting up every time we have been knocked down.

◇ ◇ ◇

When success turns your head, you're facing failure.

◇ ◇ ◇

The reward of success is opportunity.

◇ ◇ ◇

You will never reach the top of the ladder by pulling someone else down.

◇ ◇ ◇

Hard work is the tool of S-U-C-C-E-S-S.

◇ ◇ ◇

It takes more than brass to fashion the key to success.

◇ ◇ ◇

It is not so easy
   —To shoulder a deserved blame
   —To be unselfish
   —To keep on trying
BUT IT ALWAYS PAYS.

◇ ◇ ◇

Success is not a destination. It is a process.

◇ ◇ ◇

The high road to success begins at your feet.

—Harvey A. Blodgett

◇ ◇ ◇

Success simmers down to this: making the most of what you are, with what you've got.

◇ ◇ ◇

Success is making hay with the grass that grows under other people's feet.

◇ ◇ ◇

The well digger is probably the only man who can succeed in his life's work by beginning at the top.

◇ ◇ ◇

The greatest field for success is probably right where you are.

◇ ◇ ◇

The biggest block to many a man's success is his head.

◇ ◇ ◇

The surest way to get to the top is to begin at the bottom and go UP.

◇ ◇ ◇

The world is pretty much made already; success consists in adjustment.

◇ ◇ ◇

There are no elevators in the house of success. We must toil up the steps, one at a time.

◇ ◇ ◇

You won't find many success rules that'll work unless you do.

◇ ◇ ◇

Disappointment will be our portion if we expect success without effort.

◇ ◇ ◇

The best way to get to the top is by being the best man at the bottom.

—V. A. Jones

SUNDAY SCHOOL

Getting to Sunday school for some people is a case of mind over mattress.

SYMPATHY

Sympathy is two hearts tugging at one load.

TALENT
More men fail through lack of purpose than through lack of talent.

—*Billy Sunday*

◇ ◇ ◇

Whatever you have, you must either use or lose.

◇ ◇ ◇

No man needs to stand in another man's shoes; let him stand in his own.

◇ ◇ ◇

Variety of talent presents nothing but degrees of responsibility.

TEMPER
Nothing can "cook your goose" quicker than a boiling temper.

◇ ◇ ◇

Temper is one thing you can't get rid of by losing it.

◇ ◇ ◇

One thing that improves the longer you keep it—your temper.

◇ ◇ ◇

> *If you should lose your temper*
> *And you think you're a sad one,*
> *Don't ever try to find it,*
> *'Cause it must have been a bad one!*

TEMPERAMENT
A good, even temperament acts like oil on the wheels of life.

TEMPTATION

Temptations are like tramps. Treat them kindly and they return.

◇　◇　◇

When you meet temptation, turn to the right.

◇　◇　◇

On temptation: "There is always free cheese in a mouse-trap."

◇　◇　◇

Temptation can never come in such a form as to make it safe or profitable to yield.

◇　◇　◇

To withstand temptation: appropriate sustaining grace; cultivate humility which stems from a contrite heart; give yourself to God each day.

◇　◇　◇

Our only hope in overcoming temptation is to turn away at once. No dialogue with the devil. No debate with conscience. No compromise with Bible standards. No measuring yourself with others. Seek God's plan for you. "What is that to thee? follow thou me."

◇　◇　◇

Decisions leading to deterioration of our spiritual life and our God-consciousness are usually in the area of minor choices, with the almost unconscious letting down of standards. Natural desires for leisure, affluence, things, creature comforts, what the Bible calls "the cares of this world, and the deceitfulness of riches" (things).

◇　◇　◇

The safeguard against temptation: the sanctification of our desires; the thing we crave, long for.
Those disturbing desires, instincts; how deceiving, how destructive, how damning!

◇　◇　◇

Be alert for little deviations: "This won't count." It isn't always the big, crisis temptation that overthrows you; sometimes it is the least likely that is the greatest peril. Forewarned against the formidable, the obvious, it is the unlooked-for evil, the unexpected temptation that takes us by surprise.

TEN COMMANDMENTS

A west Texas small-town editor, with some space to fill, set up the Ten Commandments and ran them without comment. Seven men left town the next morning and another wrote, "Cancel my subscription; you're getting too personal."

◇　◇　◇

Above all else love God alone;
Bow down to neither wood nor stone.
God's name refuse to take in vain.
The Sabbath rest with care maintain.
Respect your parents all your days.
Hold sacred human life always.
Be loyal to your chosen mate.
Steal nothing, neither small nor great.
Report with truth your neighbor's deed;
And rid your mind of selfish greed.
　　　　　　—D. Elton Trueblood

THANKSGIVING

"I thank my God upon every remembrance of you."

◇　◇　◇

Think and thank on Thanksgiving Day.

◇　◇　◇

You'll be thankful if you are thinkful.

◇　◇　◇

He enjoys much who is thankful for a little.

◇ ◇ ◇

Thanksgiving is good—thanks-living is better. We thank Thee, Lord, for all Thy gifts.

◇ ◇ ◇

Offer unto God thanksgiving.

THOUGHT

God will not make me think like Jesus. I have to do it myself; I have to bring every thought into captivity to the obedience of Christ. "Abide in me"—in intellectual matters, in money matters, in every one of the matters that make human life what it is.

—Oswald Chambers

◇ ◇ ◇

Action without thought is like shooting without aim.

◇ ◇ ◇

You have to think STRAIGHT before you can be STRAIGHT.

◇ ◇ ◇

Opportunities of doing a kindness are often lost from mere want of thought.

◇ ◇ ◇

The happiness of your life depends upon the quality of your thoughts.

◇ ◇ ◇

Let your food for thought always contain the element of goodness.

TIME

Time is a sacred trust. "Now is the day of salvation."

◇ ◇ ◇

Give God an hour and you will be well repaid.

◇ ◇ ◇

Lost time is never found.

◇ ◇ ◇

Take time to be holy.

◇ ◇ ◇

Time comes our way but once and is gone.

◇ ◇ ◇

Killing time is not murder—it's suicide!

◇ ◇ ◇

Blessed is the man whose watch keeps church time as well as business time.

◇ ◇ ◇

Counting time is not nearly as important as making time count.

◇ ◇ ◇

Time is just a slice cut out of eternity. Where will you spend eternity?

◇ ◇ ◇

> *I have only just a minute,*
> *Only 60 seconds in it.*
> *Forced upon me—can't refuse it;*
> *Didn't seek it, didn't choose it.*
> *I must suffer if I lose it,*
> *Give account if I abuse it.*
> *Just a tiny little minute,*
> *But eternity is in it.*

TITHING

John D. Rockefeller is said to have once made the following statement concerning the habit of tithing: "I never would have been able to tithe the first million dollars I made if I had not tithed my first salary, which was $1.50 a week."

◇ ◇ ◇

Tithing is the proof that we really believe in stewardship.

◇ ◇ ◇

It is very remarkable that so few people quit tithing because it has not worked.

◇ ◇ ◇

Four *S*'s of Tithing—
(1) Scriptural, (2) Simple, (3) Sensible, (4) Serviceable.

◇ ◇ ◇

Few tithers ever give up the habit after it has become a habit.

TODAY

Don't let yesterday use up too much of today.

◇ ◇ ◇

Choose wisely today for satisfactory tomorrows.

◇ ◇ ◇

I have seen yesterday; I do not fear tomorrow; I love today!

◇ ◇ ◇

"Yesterday is gone; tomorrow is uncertain; today is here. Use it!"

◇ ◇ ◇

You have today! Take it and make the most of it.

◇ ◇ ◇

When we do our best today, we set the stage for doing better tomorrow.

◇ ◇ ◇

Regard this day as a new opportunity for service.

◇ ◇ ◇

Yesterday—a cancelled check
Tomorrow—a promissory note
Today—is ready cash. Spend it wisely.

◇ ◇ ◇

Today is the tomorrow you worried about yesterday.

◇　◇　◇

If today is one of your best days, make tomorrow just like it.

TOLERANCE
It is much easier to expect tolerance than it is to extend tolerance.

TOMORROW
Put off until tomorrow what you ought not to do at all.

—Poor Richard, Jr.

◇　◇　◇

You're not old unless you have no plans for tomorrow.

◇　◇　◇

Don't brag about what you're going to do tomorrow; somebody might ask you what you did today.

◇　◇　◇

Never forget that if we put God first, no matter what happens today, God's tomorrow can be glorious.

◇　◇　◇

What you shall be tomorrow depends largely on what you are today.

◇　◇　◇

Every tomorrow has two handles—you may grasp by the handle of anxiety or by the handle of faith.

◇　◇　◇

Fear not tomorrow—God is already there.

◇　◇　◇

Worry pulls tomorrow's cloud on today's bright sunshine.

THE TONGUE

A blunt tongue sometimes makes a sharp cut.

◇   ◇   ◇

A "bit of love" is the only "bit" that will bridle the tongue.

◇   ◇   ◇

A loose tongue often gets its owner into a tight place.

◇   ◇   ◇

"Keep thy tongue from evil, and thy lips from speaking guile."

◇   ◇   ◇

A fool's tongue is always long enough to hang himself with.

◇   ◇   ◇

Give not your tongue too much liberty or it will take you prisoner.

◇   ◇   ◇

Learn to avoid nasty remarks.

◇   ◇   ◇

To speak kindly does not hurt the tongue.

◇   ◇   ◇

A sharp tongue is no indication of a keen mind.

◇   ◇   ◇

Keep a skid chain on your tongue.

◇   ◇   ◇

Too many of us speak twice before we think.

TONGUES

A good many people have prayed for the gift of tongues who needed the gift of silence.

TRIALS/ADVERSITY

You are not the best Christian when you are exuberantly

happy in a religious service. You are most Christian when you are holding steady under pressure.

—*Bertha Munro*

◇   ◇   ◇

I need Thee. When I am lonely, forgotten, Thou art ever present. When strength fails and when overwhelmed by weariness, Thou art the Source of inspiration and renewed purpose to the steadfast and faithful. When confused and the answer to life's quandary escapes me, Thou art the Omniscient One, the All-knowing.

◇   ◇   ◇

The anvil lasts longer than the hammer.

◇   ◇   ◇

SONG OF A BIRD IN A WINTER STORM

The soft, sweet summer was warm and glowing;
Bright were the blossoms on every bough!
I trusted Him when the roses were blooming;
I trust Him now.

Small were my faith should it weakly falter
Now that the roses have ceased to blow;
Frail were the trust that now should alter,
Doubting His love when storm clouds grow.

◇   ◇   ◇

We need to be able to say with conviction when darkness closes in, when the storm roars about us, when we are going through deep waters: "The faith that glows in my heart is not a candle. Blow on!"

◇   ◇   ◇

A doctor was once asked by a patient who had met with a serious accident, "Doctor, how long shall I have to lie here?"
The answer, "Only a day at a time," taught the patient a valuable lesson. It was the same lesson that God had

recorded for His people of all ages long before. If we are faithful for one short day, the long years will take care of themselves.

—Andrew Murray

◊ ◊ ◊

A woman had spent 26 years confined to her bed and had never crossed the threshold of her room. She said, "It comes only one day at a time and God is so good."

◊ ◊ ◊

> *God broke the years to hours and days,*
> *That hour by hour*
> *And day by day,*
> *Just going on a little way,*
> *We ought to be able all along*
> *To keep quite strong.*

◊ ◊ ◊

"As thy days, so shall thy strength be."

◊ ◊ ◊

How frail is man, how utterly dependent upon God! And when earthly things upon which we depend so much and on which we build our lives and our resources are gone, we may still have God. Health, loved ones, material possessions, all the things which make for security, may fail us but God is there waiting to be heard and sought.

—A. W. Tozer

◊ ◊ ◊

> *Think not thou canst sigh a sigh*
> *And thy Maker is not by;*
> *Think not thou canst weep a tear*
> *And thy Maker is not near.*

—A. W. Tozer

◊ ◊ ◊

Seemingly adverse circumstances, even so-called tragedies, become part of the miracles of grace by which the transforming process of growing in the image of Christ is accomplished.

◇　◇　◇

By the transforming miracle of grace a Christlike character emerges from the deadly routine of life. It is developed from (or despite) gross injustices; from bitter disappointments, crushing sorrow, cruel losses, shocking tragedy.

◇　◇　◇

The monotonous grind, the adversities, the tough situations which are all too often the regular order of life can be transformed into emotional stability, habitual poise, and steadfastness of purpose.

◇　◇　◇

The true disciple chooses neither song nor dirge, neither sunshine nor shadow, has no choice but to know his Master's will and to do it. If He appoints for us the blue waters of the lake and all the sunshine of the summer, then let us rejoice therein and not vex our souls because we know no suffering and pain. If He appoints the Via Dolorosa and sunless skies, then God make us willing to take the way because the way is His appointment. We must be in His will if we are to cooperate with Him.

—*G. Campbell Morgan*

◇　◇　◇

Storms are foreboding but they give impetus to our faith; they encourage us to seize the promises with a tighter grasp; they drive us to prayer and thereby closer to God.

◇　◇　◇

Christ is building His kingdom with earth's broken things. Men want only the strong, the successful, the victorious, the unbroken, in building their kingdoms; but God is the God of the unsuccessful, of those who have failed. Heaven is filling with earth's broken lives, and there is no bruised reed that Christ cannot take and restore to glorious blessedness and beauty. He can take the life crushed by pain or sorrow and make it into a harp whose music shall be all praise. He can lift earth's saddest failure up to heaven's glory.

—*J. R. Miller*

◇   ◇   ◇

Burdened, bewildered, beset with problems, difficulties, misunderstandings, afflictions—God cares; His heart hurts for you.

◇   ◇   ◇

Popular schools of religious thought regard religion as a push-button guarantee against the impact of life's adversity and misfortune.

◇   ◇   ◇

So it must be our care to provide for afflictions; for to prevent them altogether we cannot; but prepare for them we may, and must; to treasure up God's promises, and store our souls with grace, and spiritual comforts, and firm resolutions in God's strength to bear up and to hold on: we need to be well "shod with the preparation of the gospel of peace" (Ephesians 6:15).

—*John Bunyan in "Pilgrim's Progress"*

◇   ◇   ◇

I needed the quiet. No prison my bed, / But a beautiful valley of blessings instead— / A place to grow richer, in Jesus to hide. / I needed the quiet, so He drew me aside.

—*Alice Hansche Mortenson*

◇   ◇   ◇

My God, I have never thanked Thee for my thorns. Teach me the glory of my cross; teach me the value of my thorn.

Show me that I have climbed to Thee by the path of pain.
Show me that my tears have made my rainbow.

—*George Matheson*

◇　◇　◇

For every pain that we must bear,
For every service, every care,
　There is a reason.
But if we trust Him as we should,
All will work out for our own good;
　God knows the reason.

◇　◇　◇

The years teach much which the days never know.

—*Ralph Waldo Emerson*

◇　◇　◇

O Joy that seekest me through pain,
I cannot close my heart to Thee.
I trace the rainbow through the rain,
And feel the promise is not vain
　That morn shall tearless be.

—*George Matheson*

◇　◇　◇

We all seem to thrive on laughter but we grow only through tears.

—*Mrs. George McGovern*

◇　◇　◇

Face problems, difficulties, adversities with a positive spiritual attitude of faith, trust, confidence. "My times are in thy hands."

◇　◇　◇

Sainthood springs out of suffering.

◇　◇　◇

Things that hurt and things that mar
Shape the man for perfect praise;
Shock and strain and ruin are
Friendlier than the smiling days.

◇　◇　◇

When things go wrong, don't go with them.

◇　◇　◇

Adversity, hardship, can lead to submission, humility, reliance upon God or we can become bitter, resentful. "Think it not strange concerning the fiery trial."

◇　◇　◇

We grow strong under contrary winds.

◇　◇　◇

We must strive to transform adversity into victory.

◇　◇　◇

Hammering hardens steel but crumbles putty.

◇　◇　◇

Step on your stumbling blocks instead of falling over them.

◇　◇　◇

"When the outlook is dark, try the uplook."

◇　◇　◇

No man is ever the same after he has seen God. He sees God in prosperity, in adversity, in health, in sickness.

◇　◇　◇

"Some folks don't look up until they are flat on their backs." It is by developing inner resources that in the day of testing and adversity we are not overthrown. These inner resources are built by a daily process.

◇　◇　◇

God broke our years to hours and days, that hour by hour

and day by day we might be able to bear the burdens and meet the difficulties of life.

—*William T. McElroy*

◇ ◇ ◇

The transforming power of the gospel operates not only in conversion, in delivering from habits, but it is a sustaining power. It gives strength to overcome adversity, to surmount circumstances, to rise from ashes of failure, and to live in the beauty of holiness.

◇ ◇ ◇

Madame Guyon testified that the stones of her dismal prison cell shone like precious jewels. God was there.

◇ ◇ ◇

The living Christ abides with us. It is not a matter of days and months, of selected times and places. He is never an absentee Lord. He is our Great Companion, on the street, in the place of daily toil, in the home where clean laughter is heard, as well as the voice of prayer, in the church sanctuary on the Sabbath, and by lake and stream in vacation days, in all our contacts and relationships and with our fellowmen. He seems especially near to us in the hour of bodily anguish.

—*W. E. McCulloch*

◇ ◇ ◇

When water is most highly agitated it becomes well supplied with oxygen. Turbulences causing water to dash against rocks and dropping over falls replenish supplies of oxygen and makes streams habitable.

Life's turbulence, rightly used, does a similar thing for us. It mixes heaven into our human situations in a way that peaceful ways never do. So why not welcome obstacles to our comfort?

◇ ◇ ◇

A life which had no experience of tears would lose something of infinite value. A life which never had a problem, a faith which never had a doubt, an existence which never knew anything but luxury and comfort, would all be sadly lacking in something of infinite value.

◇　◇　◇

Those who know life best say that it can be cruel, as cruel as birth, as sorrowful as death. But to the Christian it can be eternally triumphant.

◇　◇　◇

Heat hardens clay and melts wax. Storms break spotty timber and strengthen the fiber of healthy trees.

—Francesca M. Wilson in
"In the Margins of Chaos" (Macmillan)

◇　◇　◇

In the most desolate life; in the most discouraging situation, a seed may fall and, nourished by faith, may sprout and bloom into a beautiful flower. God does send "beauty for ashes."

◇　◇　◇

When life knocks you to your knees—and it always will—you are in proper posture for prayer.

◇　◇　◇

Why must I weep when others sing?
"To test the deeps of suffering."
Why must I work while others rest?
"To spend my strength at God's request."
Why must I lose while others gain?
"To understand defeat's sharp pain."
Why must this lot of life be mine
When that which fairer seems is thine?
"Because God knows what plans for me
Shall blossom in eternity."

◇　◇　◇

266

Lord, teach us to appreciate the thorns as well as the roses.

◇ ◇ ◇

No one ever climbed a hill by looking at it.

◇ ◇ ◇

A river never stops after a fall.

◇ ◇ ◇

The right road is upgrade.

◇ ◇ ◇

When you are getting kicked from the rear it means you're in front.

—*Fulton J. Sheen*

◇ ◇ ◇

Remember—every morning is a fresh beginning.

◇ ◇ ◇

Difficulties have a way of disappearing when you laugh at them.

◇ ◇ ◇

Many voices have offered me a home for my quiet hours. Thou alone hast promised me a covert in my storm.

—*George Matheson*

◇ ◇ ◇

The stops of a good man, as well as his steps, are ordered by the Lord.

◇ ◇ ◇

Look your difficulties in the face and they will begin to run.

◇ ◇ ◇

There are no gains without pains.

◇ ◇ ◇

Remember—when in deep water, keep your mouth shut.

◇ ◇ ◇

Face your difficulties and acknowledge them; but do not let them master you.

—*Helen Keller*

◇ ◇ ◇

During trying times don't quit trying.

◇ ◇ ◇

The soul would have no rainbow had the eyes no tears.

◇ ◇ ◇

If your burdens are heavy, try kneeling under them.

◇ ◇ ◇

Fire is a test of gold; adversity, of strong men.

◇ ◇ ◇

Every difficulty is either a grindstone or a stepping-stone.

◇ ◇ ◇

To bear misfortune calmly is to have a fortune.

◇ ◇ ◇

Too much sunshine will ruin a crop.

◇ ◇ ◇

If there were no difficulties there would be no triumphs.

◇ ◇ ◇

You may stop loving God, but God never stops loving you.

◇ ◇ ◇

The gem cannot be polished without friction, nor man perfected without trials.

◇ ◇ ◇

It is not affliction itself, but affliction rightly borne, that does us good.

◇ ◇ ◇

Spread thy sails to catch the favoring breezes of adversity.

◇ ◇ ◇

A blow of misfortune may lay us low, but never beyond the care of the Heavenly Father.

◇ ◇ ◇

268

There is no good arguing with the inevitable. The only argument available with an east wind is to put on your overcoat.

—*James Russell Lowell*

◇   ◇   ◇

A brick is useless until it has been through the fire; so is a man.

◇   ◇   ◇

Often human ends are divine beginnings.

◇   ◇   ◇

Cross-bearing ends in crown-wearing.

◇   ◇   ◇

Christians are like tea—their real strength comes out when they get into hot water.

◇   ◇   ◇

Difficulties strengthen the mind as labor does the body.

◇   ◇   ◇

The proof of our faith is in the stability with which we live through the alternating circumstances which confront us— success, failure, health, illness, prosperity, financial need, popularity, ostracism.

◇   ◇   ◇

The only difference between stumbling blocks and stepping-stones is the way you use them.

◇   ◇   ◇

The walls of circumstance can shut us out of many things, but it is well to remember that they only shut us in with God.

—*C. F. Thomas*

◇   ◇   ◇

Strength comes from struggles, weakness from ease.

◇   ◇   ◇

269

Accept the bitter with the sweet and rejoice in both.

◇　◇　◇

True martyrs never remind anyone of the fact.

◇　◇　◇

Adversity makes a man wise, though not rich.

◇　◇　◇

When everything seems to be going dead wrong, take a good look and see if you are headed in the right direction.

◇　◇　◇

Hard grinds in life seem necessary. Razors can't be sharpened on velvet.

◇　◇　◇

A little talk with Jesus! How it smooths the rugged road!

◇　◇　◇

Whine less; pray more.

◇　◇　◇

Your extremity is God's opportunity. Why not try God?

TROUBLE

Jesus is not only "a very present help in trouble," but a Help in preventing trouble.

◇　◇　◇

The teakettle is up to its neck in hot water, but it sings a merry tune.

◇　◇　◇

Obstacles are put in your way to find out whether you really want a thing—or just think you do.

◇　◇　◇

Don't walk into trouble and expect God to get you out.

◇　◇　◇

Your mouth is much more likely to make trouble for you than your ears.

◇　◇　◇

You do not need bank references to borrow trouble.

◇　◇　◇

The final proof of self-control is to listen to another's troubles and say nothing about your own.

◇　◇　◇

Great pilots are made during turbulent flights.

◇　◇　◇

When you dig another out of his trouble you bury your own.

◇　◇　◇

Trouble is only opportunity in work clothes.

◇　◇　◇

The Bible contains more wisdom for troubled people than textbooks on psychology and psychiatry.

◇　◇　◇

Troubles grow by recounting them.

◇　◇　◇

You may have a heavy cross to bear along life's road, but being cross as a bear never lightens the load.

◇　◇　◇

Troubles, like babies, grow larger by nursing.

◇　◇　◇

When we sigh about our trouble, it grows double.

◇　◇　◇

Yield not in trouble to dismay. God can deliver any day.

—*Martin Luther*

◇　◇　◇

Rough paths often lead to desirable destinations.

◇　◇　◇

He that seeks trouble always finds it.

◇　◇　◇

Trouble is a great sieve through which we sift our acquaintances; those who are too big to pass through are our friends.

◇　◇　◇

We can have trouble without being defeated.

◇　◇　◇

Most of our troubles are caused by too much bone in the head and not enough in the back.

◇　◇　◇

Learn to keep your troubles to yourself; nobody wants them.

◇　◇　◇

All sunshine makes the desert.

◇　◇　◇

I have never met a man who has given me as much trouble as myself.

—*Dwight L. Moody*

TRUST

Though vine nor fig tree neither
Their wonted fruit should bear,
Though all the field should wither,
Nor flocks nor herds be there;
Yet, God the same abiding,
His praise shall tune my voice,
For while in Him confiding,
I cannot but rejoice.

—*William Cowper*

◇　◇　◇

In a time of turmoil like the present the need of the individual soul is to lay hold upon fundamental things, one of which is trust in the power and goodness of God. In our age many of the things in which men have trusted have been shaken. But there are "things that cannot be shaken," and these are still available to us, if we have eyes to see them and faith to grasp them. The God who has guided the world in the past is still in control. When the "tumult" and the "shouting" have died and the "captains" and the "kings" have departed, He will still be "our refuge and strength."

◇   ◇   ◇

Trust: a body relaxed, a mind at peace, a heart at rest.

◇   ◇   ◇

Cast all your cares on God. That anchor *holds*.

◇   ◇   ◇

Trust in God, and you are never to be confounded in time or eternity!

◇   ◇   ◇

God will not let you down if you trust and obey.

◇   ◇   ◇

I do not see my way; but I know that He sees His way, and that I see Him.

—*Charles Kingsley*

◇   ◇   ◇

It is a little thing to trust God as far as we can see Him, so far as the way lies open before us; but to trust in Him when we are hedged in on every side and can see no way to escape, this is good and acceptable with God.

—*John Wesley*

◇   ◇   ◇

Father is with us; we are unafraid. This is the deeper meaning of being children of God—unreserved committal and a childlike trust. "I will fear no evil: for thou art with me."

TRUTH

When our minds are conditioned by prejudice or paralyzed

by traditional views, we may face a truth in scripture again and again without its ever touching us. Our spiritual inhibition concerning that truth permits us to see, but not to perceive. The truth lies dormant within, mentally apprehended but not spiritually applied.

◇　◇　◇

There is nothing so powerful as truth, and nothing so strange.

◇　◇　◇

Some people have the ability to so twist the gospel truth that it loses its meaning.

◇　◇　◇

Truth is the highest thing man can keep.

◇　◇　◇

The truth doesn't hurt unless it ought to.

◇　◇　◇

Truth never walks on crutches.

◇　◇　◇

When a fellow has a reputation for telling the truth he doesn't have to prove everything he says.

◇　◇　◇

Some people, in applying for a job, ask their preacher to recommend them, and some are willing that he should tell the truth.

◇　◇　◇

There is very little truth in a half-truth.

◇　◇　◇

The truth is always the strongest argument.

◇　◇　◇

It is easy to think we have been abused when we have been compelled to listen to the truth.

◇　◇　◇

Truth is often eclipsed but never extinguished.

◇   ◇   ◇

A grain of truth beats a bushel of bunk.

◇   ◇   ◇

The fact is that truth is your best friend, no matter what the circumstances are.

—*Abraham Lincoln*

UNANSWERED PRAYER

Jesus never answers when your mind is all made up. He is always silent before the inquiry of one who has already made up his mind.

◇   ◇   ◇

Some prayers are unanswered because they have been thought about, but never really expressed to God.

◇   ◇   ◇

Let us distinguish between unfulfilled wishes and unanswered prayer.

UNITY

Man struggles in various ways, by human means, to restore the unity that has been lost in the church. But forces and systems and organization have failed to accomplish this. Polish and technique and ritual, in their tragic failure, only serve to accent the chaos of divisiveness and disunity caused by sin.

—*John A. Mackay*

◇   ◇   ◇

If creeds divide, let deeds unite.

◇   ◇   ◇

There is so much that divides us these days. There are far too many fences and not enough bridges. It has often been said that if we don't know how to bury our prejudices here we will have a rough time of it in heaven. The Christian fellowship seeks to be inclusive, not exclusive. It must draw others into the fellowship, not push them out. It must provide an open door, not a barricade.

—*J. Fred Parker*

◇　◇　◇

There can be no racial, social, economic, or intellectual differences great enough to justify separation between those who have experienced divine life through Christ.

VACATION
No matter where you spend your vacation, God is there.

VIRTUE
A thankful heart is not only the greatest virtue, but the parent of all other virtues.

◇　◇　◇

The day will come again when thrift will be considered a virtue.

VISION
Poor eyes limit a man's sight; poor vision, his deeds.

WALKING
By walking straight you get into the best circles.

WAR
We have war because men refuse to accept the Prince of Peace.

WEAKNESS

Even the best of us comes far short of God's ideal. All therefore are in need of His help and grace. None of us ever goes beyond that point of need.

◇ ◇ ◇

God knows both our weakness and our strength. He never overloads anybody.

◇ ◇ ◇

It is a positive crime to be weak in God's strength.

—*Oswald Chambers*

◇ ◇ ◇

Love strengthens the weak.

◇ ◇ ◇

It takes a long time to build up a good name, but it can be lost in a moment of weakness.

WILL OF GOD

If you wish to keep Christ very near you, and to feel Him near you, the way to do so is no mere cultivation of religious emotion or saturating your mind with religious books and thoughts, though these have their place; but on the dusty road of life doing His will and keeping His commandments.

—*Alexander Maclaren*

◇ ◇ ◇

The will of God: nothing more, nothing less, nothing else.

◇ ◇ ◇

Obedience to the known will of God—that is the secret of Christian progress.

—*O. P. Gifford*

◇ ◇ ◇

If you abide in the will of God, you will have an experience that will abide.

WISDOM

Wisdom is knowing what to do next; skill is knowing how to do it; virtue is doing it.

◇　◇　◇

Wisdom consists in knowing what to do with what you know.

◇　◇　◇

Seek wisdom and guidance from God, that you may avoid life's pitfalls.

◇　◇　◇

You may attain to wisdom if you have not assumed that you already possess it.

◇　◇　◇

Knowledge is taking things apart; wisdom is putting them back together.

WITNESS

Heaven's gate is shut to him who comes alone.

◇　◇　◇

If there is no desperation in your witnessing, if there is a take-it-or-leave-it air, you haven't experienced what the Psalmist felt when he said, "For the zeal of thy house has consumed me" (Ps. 69:9, RSV).

◇　◇　◇

If more saints would learn the meaning of the word *GO*, more sinners would heed the call, *COME*.

◇　◇　◇

The torch of religion may be lighted in the church, but it does its burning in the shop and on the street.

◇　◇　◇

The Christ we do not share, we do not keep.

◇　◇　◇

Let your life and lips express
The holy gospel you profess.

◇ ◇ ◇

Blair Quick, a businessman in Cleveland, had been a great blessing in his church and community. One day the Lord spoke to him: "Go out and use your talents for Me." He protested: "But, Lord, I have no talents." Christ replied, "You have 10 talents. You have a heart to let Me dwell in; that's one. You have two ears to listen to My voice; that makes three. You have two eyes to look for men for Me; that makes five. You have two feet to walk for Me; that makes seven. You have two hands to reach out to your fellows for Me; that makes nine. And you have a mouth to testify for My glory. Go out and use your 10 talents for Me."

◇ ◇ ◇

You may be inexperienced; you may shrink from personal encounters; you may not be gifted with ready speech; you may not be versed in doctrinal truth. But you have been redeemed; your sins have been forgiven; your life has been transformed; your hope is in the God of your salvation. Tell the good news to others!

◇ ◇ ◇

Whittaker Chambers defines a witness as "a man whose life and faith are so completely one that when the challenge comes to step out and testify for his faith he does so, disregarding all risks, accepting all consequences."

◇ ◇ ◇

Too many people luxuriate in the peace Christ has given, neglecting the sober thinking which an evil age requires. And so we have people glibly testifying to saving grace who have very dull ethical and social consciences.

◇ ◇ ◇

279

Beware of any society in which you feel compelled to put a bushel over your testimony.

◇ ◇ ◇

If you are to be a shining light, there must be some fire back of it.

◇ ◇ ◇

If our Christian light is curtailed, it is not because of a power shortage.

◇ ◇ ◇

He who whispers down a well
About the goods he has to sell
Will never make as many dollars
As he who climbs a tree and hollers.

◇ ◇ ◇

Witnessing for Christ should start at home.

◇ ◇ ◇

Take Christ with you as a Friend and, when you meet anyone, introduce Him.

WORDS

Praise on the tombstone does not scratch out harsh words spoken in a lifetime.

◇ ◇ ◇

Never let an opportunity pass to say a kind word to someone.

◇ ◇ ◇

A moment of thought is worth an hour of words.

◇ ◇ ◇

The man of few words doesn't have to take so many of them back.

◇ ◇ ◇

Words break no bones; *hearts* though, sometimes.

—*Robert Browning*

◇ ◇ ◇

Of the 600,000 words in the English language, here are the most important: *I am proud of you; What is your opinion? If you please; Thank you.* The least important is *I*—yet we use it 450 times more than any of the others.

◇　◇　◇

Big men use little words; little men use big words.

◇　◇　◇

Let us translate our words into deeds.

WORK

The test of a vocation is the love of the drudgery it involves.

◇　◇　◇

A thing done right today means less trouble tomorrow.

◇　◇　◇

The dignity of labor depends, not on what you do, but on how you do it.

◇　◇　◇

My work is my blessing, not my doom.

◇　◇　◇

Three men were fired: Bullheaded Ben, Sloppy Sam, and Thickheaded Theodore.

◇　◇　◇

The clock attracts attention because its hands are never idle.

◇　◇　◇

Your work should be a challenge, not a chore.

◇　◇　◇

In a labor of love, every day is payday.

◇　◇　◇

It's not the load that breaks you down! It's the way you carry it.

◇　◇　◇

The place a man occupies is never as important as the work he does.

◇　◇　◇

The greatest comfort is the knowledge that you are doing your job well.

◇　◇　◇

One doesn't advance in any field on standard working hours.

◇　◇　◇

I have seen many a self-made man who I think knocked off work too soon.

◇　◇　◇

To leave footprints on the sands of time, wear work shoes.

◇　◇　◇

Business is exactly like a wheelbarrow—if you don't push it, it won't go.

◇　◇　◇

WOULD-BE EMPLOYER: "Have you any references?"
WOULD-BE EMPLOYEE: "Sure, here's the letter: 'To whom it may concern, John Jones worked for us one week, and we're satisfied.'"

◇　◇　◇

One reason opportunity isn't recognized more often is that it goes around disguised as work.

◇　◇　◇

Plain hard work would cure most of our ills but it is a price few of us want to pay.

WORLD

The gospel is at its best when the world is at its worst.

◇　◇　◇

Almost half of the world's 3 billion people go to bed hungry as "their sob follows the sun around the globe." During the

282

past 30 seconds 20 people have died of hunger; 10,000 people, according to one estimate, die of starvation every day. In India alone, 50 million children will die of malnutrition in the next 10 years. And it costs a million dollars a day to store the excess of our crops! *(Editor's note: Statistics may become outdated, but in this case it would simply be a case of increase at every point.)*

◇ ◇ ◇

*The great world's heart is aching, aching fiercely in the
    night;
And God alone can heal it, and God alone give light.
And the men to bear that message and to speak the living
    Word
Are you and I, my brothers, and the millions who have
    heard.*
—Frederick George Scott

◇ ◇ ◇

The world's problems will never be solved—war, crimes, poverty, racism, political graft and corruption—as long as men themselves remain unchanged. It would be as futile, says Dr. Sockman, as trying to calm a storm at sea by skimming off the whitecaps.

◇ ◇ ◇

What the world needs is conviction instead of conformity, commitment instead of compromise.

◇ ◇ ◇

If we wish to make the world a new one, we have the materials ready. The first one was made out of chaos.

◇ ◇ ◇

Men who have much to say use the fewest words.
—H. W. Shaw

◇ ◇ ◇

The world is taking your picture. Look pleasant, please.

◇　◇　◇

Start to reform the world in your own heart.

◇　◇　◇

Laugh and the world laughs with you; cry and you cry alone.

◇　◇　◇

A lot of people are so busy telling the world what is wrong with it they do not have the time to do anything about it.

◇　◇　◇

No one ever solves the hurt of the world by feeling sorry for himself.

◇　◇　◇

The world could have been redeemed long ago if money could have done it without a little personal help from the givers.

◇　◇　◇

This world will never be saved by programs, but we will never save the world unless we have a program.

WORLDLINESS

Don't go where you would not be willing to die.

◇　◇　◇

The world is full of men who are making good livings, but poor lives.

◇　◇　◇

God left out of human affairs spells disaster.

◇　◇　◇

Unless there is within us that which is above us, we shall soon yield to that which is about us.

◇　◇　◇

People cannot understand our protests against worldliness

of one sort when we are so oblivious of worldliness of another, greater sort.

◇ ◇ ◇

Worldliness is the practice of the absence of God.

◇ ◇ ◇

The "world" is society organized apart from God.

◇ ◇ ◇

Worldliness is a spirit, a temperament, an attitude of soul. It is life without high callings, life devoid of lofty ideals. It is a horizontal gaze, never vertical. Its goal is success, not holiness. God is not denied; He is forgotten and ignored.

—J. H. Jowett

◇ ◇ ◇

Unless day by day the spirit is renewed by fresh visitation from God, the soul will by an almost imperceptible process be pressed into the world mold. Be transformed by the divine companionship.

—Oliver G. Wilson

WORRY

Bishop Quayle sat up one night worrying. Finally God spoke to him and said, "You had better go to bed, Quayle; I'll sit up the rest of the night."

◇ ◇ ◇

Worry is a sneak thief. Trust God.

◇ ◇ ◇

Some people develop eyestrain looking for trouble.

◇ ◇ ◇

Worry often gives a small thing a big shadow.

◇ ◇ ◇

Fix, establish in your mind the idea that God is there. If once the mind is centered in that truth, then when you are

in difficulties it is as easy as breathing to remember—
Why, my Father knows all about it! It is not an effort, it
comes naturally when perplexities press. *God is my Father; He loves me.* I shall never think of anything He will
forget or in which He is not interested or involved, so why
should I worry?

◇　◇　◇

Worrying is just a habit that you have learned.

◇　◇　◇

The fat man can lose weight; the drunk can sober up; but
the Christian can't quit worrying!

◇　◇　◇

Worrying about nothing but pray about everything.

◇　◇　◇

Worry is like a rocking chair—it will give you something to
do, but it won't get you anywhere.

◇　◇　◇

The worst thing about crossing a bridge before you get to
it is that it leaves you on the wrong side of the river.

◇　◇　◇

Worry is the advance interest you pay on troubles that
seldom come.

◇　◇　◇

Why worry because your hair is falling out? Suppose it
ached and you had to have it pulled, like your teeth?

◇　◇　◇

Worry has never been able to stand up against laughter.

◇　◇　◇

Anxiety never yet successfully bridged over any chasm.

◇　◇　◇

To carry care to bed is to sleep with a pack on your back.

◇　◇　◇

When you get all wrinkled with worry and care, it's time to get your faith lifted.

◇　◇　◇

You can't change the past, but you can ruin a perfectly good present worrying about the future.

◇　◇　◇

Worry leaves when trust in God comes in.

◇　◇　◇

Try to remember some of the things you were worrying about last week.

◇　◇　◇

Worry is the most popular form of suicide.

◇　◇　◇

If you can pray, why worry?

◇　◇　◇

Some people major in minor things.

WORSHIP

Worship renews the spirit as sleep renews the body.

◇　◇　◇

The worship most acceptable to God comes from a thankful and cheerful heart.

◇　◇　◇

Somewhere, even when duties are most grinding, and the pressure of obligations most severe, there is a burning bush nearby. Then we remove our shoes, for we are on holy ground. We worship. The glory of God's presence transforms our lives with heavenly radiance.

◇　◇　◇

The Most High is not deceived nor pleased with unworthy worship. He has said some very stern and solemn things about that in His Word. He will make allowances for immaturity and inexperience, but not for carelessness, fri-

287

volity, or cheapness. One of the things most greatly needed in our churches today—and in our hearts—is an uplifting and a heart-humbling sense of God.

—*R. W. Graves*

◇   ◇   ◇

"We are a nervous, taut, hard-pressed, easily upset, easily irritated, and easily exhausted generation," said Dr. Harold Bosley. To that we might add, *without inner resources, because we fail to worship.*

◇   ◇   ◇

When we go to church and fail to participate and respond in our group worship, there is no reverence in our hearts.

◇   ◇   ◇

When awe of God is gone, there can be no true worship.

◇   ◇   ◇

Worship is man's answer to God's call.

◇   ◇   ◇

We worship wherever and whenever we are aware of God.

◇   ◇   ◇

The full rewards of worship are bestowed only on the soul which actively communes with God.

◇   ◇   ◇

Worship reminds us of who we are and whom we serve. In worship we refer our lives to God. Worship reminds us that God's thoughts and ways are not ours. It does not take God for granted, but draws us to Him with a sort of humble confidence. It is a confrontation with God apart from which we are not truly able to confront the world.

—*Wilbur C. Lamm*

◇   ◇   ◇

I went with the multitude to the house of God on the Sabbath day. I learned it was a place of worship; I knelt reverently and prayed. A feeling of calm came over me;

peace lingered with me; fear assuaged, courage revived, faith strengthened, hope was renewed, love was born, and God became real to me.

—*Benjamin Litelgeroge*

◇　◇　◇

In our worship we may see God as He is—ready and waiting to renew; to quicken, restore, cleanse, energize, enlarge our capacities, deepen our compassion for those in need.

◇　◇　◇

True worship is listening for the heavenly voice. It means shutting ourselves alone with Him, just waiting in the sacred silence for the music of His voice. But listening takes time. And our worship is tragically lacking because we give so little time to it. How foolish! How shortsighted! When God has abundant supply for our every need; when He has the solution to our every problem!

◇　◇　◇

Forms of worship are empty shells. Real worship is an experience of God. Without God in it, worship is dead.

◇　◇　◇

To worship is to quicken the conscience by the holiness of God, to feed the mind with the truth of God, to purge the imagination by the beauty of God, to open the heart to the love of God, to devote the will to the purpose of God. All this is gathered up in the emotion which most cleanses us from selfishness because it is the most selfless of all emotions—worship.

—*William Temple*

◇　◇　◇

We have wandered far afield if what Vance Havner said is true of our worship: "There is nothing about us to suggest that we have been looking at anything stupendous and overwhelming."

◇　◇　◇

To worship is to be overwhelmed by the greatness and glory of God.

—*C. Neil Strait*

◇　◇　◇

Participation is so important in communal worship! One joins in the hymn singing (on key or off); the scripture lesson and the pastoral prayer are carefully followed. And the sermon, be it powerful or somewhat wanting in strength, is still the message of God delivered through His servant. Heed it! Physical and mental discipline are effective at this point.

◇　◇　◇

It takes time to be holy. A devotional spirit is essential to real worship, and such a spirit must be cultivated. Cultivation means care, nourishment, safeguarding. Worship isn't had without a price—preparation.

◇　◇　◇

When we truly worship, we forget the clamor of self-centered interests. We thrust aside nagging cares and annoying perplexities. We are transported in spirit to a world of transcendent calm, of quiet security, of perfect peace, of satisfying assurance. We worship.

◇　◇　◇

We should go to church to worship God; try to shut out the world and think only of the Lord, the message brought by the minister, and our own need of God.

YOUTH

Behind the flimsy front of rebellion and protest among so many young people is an innate aversion to restraint and control.

◇　◇　◇

No father has a right to complain about his boy going to the devil if he has never taken his boy to Sunday school.

◇　◇　◇

A very large percentage of juvenile delinquency originates in parental delinquency.

◇   ◇   ◇

Our nation and the world go forward or slip backward on the feet of the youth and children of today. And we are responsible how they go.

◇   ◇   ◇

Better build a boy than mend a man.

◇   ◇   ◇

A child that learns to cope by taking tranquilizers will grow up and cope by popping pills.

◇   ◇   ◇

America's number one drug problem is not LSD, but alcohol.

◇   ◇   ◇

A teen-ager once said, "I was thinking about my parents and how they messed things up and had done such a terrible job with the world in their generation. And then it hit me: If they are all that bad, how come I'm such a wonderful guy?"

—Charlie Shedd

ZEAL

Zeal, apart from love, is frequently intolerant and unmerciful.

FOREIGN PROVERBS*

Compassion is not just for another; it circles round and is for me.—*Japan.*

◇   ◇   ◇

Big words never broke a man's jawbone.—*Belize.*

◇   ◇   ◇

A rope is made up of many small fibers.—*Latin America.*

◇   ◇   ◇

God squeezes but He doesn't strangle.—*Uruguay.*

◇   ◇   ◇

Two bulls can't live in the same pen.—*Swaziland.*

◇   ◇   ◇

To know the road ahead, ask those coming back.—*Taiwan.*

◇   ◇   ◇

A mud turtle is never roasted (said of task impossible to get done).—*Africa.*

◇   ◇   ◇

God gives the shoulder according to the burden.—*Germany.*

◇   ◇   ◇

Since the excuse was invented, nobody has been wrong.—*Peru.*

◇   ◇   ◇

Looking for a fish? Don't climb a tree.—*Taiwan.*

◇   ◇   ◇

*Many of the proverbs in this section appeared for the first time in the *Other Sheep,* foreign missions publication of the Church of the Nazarene.

He who dresses in that which does not belong to him may be stripped when he goes out into the street.—*Uruguay*.

◇ ◇ ◇

When cockroaches give a party they don't invite fowl. (Be careful how you choose your friends.)—*Jamaica*.

◇ ◇ ◇

Fear makes the wolf bigger than he is.—*Germany*.

◇ ◇ ◇

Every vendor claims his own beans are the best available (on pride).—*Arabic*.

◇ ◇ ◇

To be happy is to be sweet inside.—*Nigeria*.

◇ ◇ ◇

All matters finish by talking.—*Africa*.

◇ ◇ ◇

If the Lord is Lord, then it follows to follow.—*Japan*.

◇ ◇ ◇

No sword blade is a match for compassion. (Love disarms enmity.)—*Japan*

◇ ◇ ◇

Only God is perfect (excusing one's mistakes).—*Arabic*.

◇ ◇ ◇

He jus' han' napkin turn teble clot' (said of a person who puts on airs).—*Belize*.

◇ ◇ ◇

There is no distinction of upper-lower in love.—*Japan*.

◇ ◇ ◇

He feels the bite of the snake. (He's hungry.)—*Africa*.

◇ ◇ ◇

The dog barks but the caravan moves on.—*Arabic*.

◇ ◇ ◇

Baboons laugh at each others' receding foreheads.—*Africa.*

◇   ◇   ◇

The beggar and the mouse, never show them the door to your house! (unwelcome callers).—*Arabic.*

◇   ◇   ◇

One generation plants the trees; another gets the shade.—*China.*

◇   ◇   ◇

The polecat doesn't smell itself.—*Africa.*

◇   ◇   ◇

Can there be smoke from a fireless chimney?—*Korea.*

◇   ◇   ◇

To stand softly is better than to beg pardon.—*Belize.*

◇   ◇   ◇

If you put your ear to a mangrove root, you'll hear a crab cough.—*Virgin Islands.*

◇   ◇   ◇

A man never steps into the same river twice.—*China.*

◇   ◇   ◇

The hay does not eat the horse.—*Africa.*

◇   ◇   ◇

Even a dog may look at the governor.—*Jamaica.*

◇   ◇   ◇

Can a man look into a person as he looks into an open-weave basket?—*Africa.*

◇   ◇   ◇

Better to eat a dry crust of bread with peace of mind than have a banquet in a house full of trouble.—*Israel.*

◇   ◇   ◇

Don't laugh at old age—pray to reach it, too.—*Taiwan.*

◇   ◇   ◇

It is hard for an empty sack to stand straight.—*Japan.*

◇   ◇   ◇

In a court of birds a worm never wins his case.—*Africa.*

◇　◇　◇

Two good talkers are not worth one good listener.—*Taiwan.*

◇　◇　◇

If a ruler pays attention to false information, all his officials will be liars.—*Israel.*

◇　◇　◇

He who climbs on the tiger's back can't choose the place to dismount.—*Africa.*

◇　◇　◇

The lion has begotten a hyena (said of a son who has proven unworthy).—*Africa.*

◇　◇　◇

I heard it through a termite hole (learned a secret).—*Africa.*

◇　◇　◇

One family builds the wall—two families enjoy it.—*Taiwan.*

◇　◇　◇

Nebba buy puss eena bag.—*Jamaica.*

◇　◇　◇

Flies don't enter a closed mouth.—*Uruguay*

◇　◇　◇

Serve fresh buttermilk to the newcomer, but don't neglect the one who's been around awhile (buttermilk being a delicacy).—*Arabic.*

◇　◇　◇

Never throw a rat into a bin of peanuts.—*Africa.*

◇　◇　◇

A person near ink gets black.—*Korea.*

◇　◇　◇

If a crab waits, he loses his head. (He who hesitates is lost.)
—*Barbados.*

◇　◇　◇

It isn't for want of a tongue that a bull doesn't talk.—*Virgin Islands.*

◇　◇　◇

Some people see the sky through a funnel.—*Japan.*

◇　◇　◇

A hoe is bought by seeing it.—*Zulu.*

◇　◇　◇

When a fish comes from the river bottom and says that the alligator has a stomachache, believe him—*Belize.*

◇　◇　◇

Like waiting for a pig to fly.—*Japan.*

◇　◇　◇

The beauty of man lies in the eloquence of his tongue.—*Arabic.*

◇　◇　◇

After the march, the trumpet sounds.—*Korea.*

◇　◇　◇

Loose goat can't tell what tied goat sees.—*Barbados.*

◇　◇　◇

Don't make a needle into a pestle *(heavy stick used in pounding out grain).* (Don't make a mountain out of a molehill.)—*Korea.*

◇　◇　◇

The weasel is at ease when the mamba [snake] has gone out.—*Zulu.*

◇　◇　◇

Your head isn't made for a hat alone.—*Barbados.*

◇　◇　◇

Time is longer than rope.—*Belize.*

◇　◇　◇

Mercy is with God and action is with man.—*Philippines.*

◇ ◇ ◇

You can bury a dog's tail for three years and it will not grow weasel's fur.—*Korea.*

◇ ◇ ◇

A child relies on its mother for courage.—*Africa.*

◇ ◇ ◇

Don't push your head in where your body can't go.—*Barbados.*

◇ ◇ ◇

The storm makes oak trees take deeper root.—*Japan.*

◇ ◇ ◇

Help thy brother's boat across, and, lo, thine own hath reached the shore.—*India.*

◇ ◇ ◇

A pumpkin will never bear watermelons.—*Belize.*

◇ ◇ ◇

Even though the bees bite me, I will take the honey (expressing determination to do a difficult thing).—*Mozambique.*

◇ ◇ ◇

An empty bag can't stand up, and a full bag can't bend.—*Barbados.*

◇ ◇ ◇

If the rain wets your buddy today, don't laugh. Today for me, tomorrow for you.—*Virgin Islands.*

◇ ◇ ◇

Like a monkey out of his tree.—*Japan.*

◇ ◇ ◇

He who steals a needle will become a cow thief.—*Korea.*

◇ ◇ ◇

The more things change, the more they are the same.—*France.*

◇ ◇ ◇

Never call the alligator "big mouth" until you have finished crossing the river.—*Belize.*

◇ ◇ ◇

A vile rat sitting on a beautiful vase can't be killed.—*Mozambique.*

◇ ◇ ◇

Don't put a cat to watch butter.—*Barbados.*

◇ ◇ ◇

When a man is dead, grass grows to his door.—*Virgin Islands.*

◇ ◇ ◇

Where might is master, justice is servant.—*Japan.*

◇ ◇ ◇

A small garden has bitter weeds.—*Barbados.*

◇ ◇ ◇

Bushes have ears and jalousies (shutters) have eyes.—*Virgin Islands.*

◇ ◇ ◇

Too much hurry, get dey tomorra. Tek time, get dey tiday.—*Belize.*

◇ ◇ ◇

One rat in the roof-grass uncovers many more in the rubbish heap close by. (Evils don't exist singly.)—*Mozambique.*

◇ ◇ ◇

It's a bad thing when dishcloth turn tablecloth.—*Virgin Islands.*

◇ ◇ ◇

Women and small men are hard to manage.—*Japan.*

◇ ◇ ◇

When a big man is in trouble, a little boy's trousers will fit him.—*Barbados.*

◇ ◇ ◇

One bracelet alone cannot jingle.—*Lebowa people, Africa.*

◇　◇　◇

Every day is fishing day, but not every day is catching day.—*Virgin Islands.*

◇　◇　◇

Dust collected becomes a mountain.—*Japan.*

◇　◇　◇

The grasshopper climbs the highest mountain by little jumps.—*Mozambique.*

◇　◇　◇

Every skin-teet (grin) ain' a laugh.—*Barbados.*

◇　◇　◇

Too much humility is pride.—*Japan.*

◇　◇　◇

It tek one finger to feel a louse, but two to tek it out.—*Barbados.*

◇　◇　◇

He who asks no questions gets only beeswax to eat.—*Mozambique.*

◇　◇　◇

New broom sweep clean, but old broom knows where the dirt lies.—*Virgin Islands.*

◇　◇　◇

He caused me to hold up a wall. (He deceived me.)—*Zulu.*

◇　◇　◇

It takes a tall mountain to cast a long shadow.—*Korea.*

◇　◇　◇

Even a fish head becomes an object of worship.—*Japan.*

◇　◇　◇

Better ask twice before you lose your way once.—*Denmark.*

◇　◇　◇

300

When rain come, John Crow says he will build a house.—*Belize.*

◇ ◇ ◇

Don't be like the hyena that split in the middle. (He smelled a goat on one side and a pig on the other, and trying to get both, he split; i.e., suffered from a divided heart.)—*Mozambique.*

◇ ◇ ◇

The zebra has no horns because it sent for them instead of going itself.—*Tsonga, Africa.*

◇ ◇ ◇

What a man doesn't know is older than he is.—*Jamaica.*

◇ ◇ ◇

The lazy ox drinks dirty water.—*Uruguay.*

◇ ◇ ◇

You can hide and buy land, but you can't hide and work it.—*Trinidad.*

◇ ◇ ◇

One bird in the hand is worth a hundred flying.—*Uruguay.*

◇ ◇ ◇

Don't bring a crocodile into your village.—*Mozambique.*

◇ ◇ ◇

The earth has ears and the news has wings.—*Philippines.*

◇ ◇ ◇

Be content with mackerel and sprat, because sometimes you can't get even that.—*Virgin Islands.*

◇ ◇ ◇

The feast is due to its owner. (The man responsible must accept the responsibility.)—*Zulu.*

◇ ◇ ◇

One li off the road will become a thousand li.—*Korea.*

◇ ◇ ◇

Getting up early doesn't make the day any longer.— *Uruguay.*

◇   ◇   ◇

If you lie with dogs, you will get up with fleas.—*Jamaica.*

◇   ◇   ◇

A snake that you see does not bite.—*Tsonga, Africa.*

◇   ◇   ◇

The nail that sticks out gets hammered down.—*Japan.*

◇   ◇   ◇

He who reaches around a lot cannot squeeze very tight.— *Republic of South Africa.*

◇   ◇   ◇

When you're digging a trap (pit), you dig one for yourself. —*Jamaica.*

◇   ◇   ◇

He put a finger into his own eye.—*Zulu.*

◇   ◇   ◇

Every man knows where his own house leaks.—*Belize.*

◇   ◇   ◇

In easy times, we forget even incense. . . . Come hard times, we embrace the Buddha's feet.—*Taiwan.*

◇   ◇   ◇

Back of dog is dog; front of dog is "Mister Dog." (Subservience shouldn't be mistaken for respect.)—*Jamaica.*

◇   ◇   ◇

A stranger's feet should be small. (Don't push yourself forward when you are in a new group.)—*Africa.*

◇   ◇   ◇

In a multitude of words there are sure to be mistakes.— *Taiwan.*

◇   ◇   ◇

Many molehills make a great mountain.—*Korea.*

◇   ◇   ◇

Don't ignore the scrawny cow in the pasture—she might be the bull's mother.—*Jamaica.*

◇ ◇ ◇

Divide an orange; it tastes just as good.—*Taiwan.*

◇ ◇ ◇

Whatever can't catch you can't pass you.—*West Indies.*

◇ ◇ ◇

A sleeping dog doesn't catch the hare.—*Africa.*

◇ ◇ ◇

He's too poor to paint and too proud to whitewash.—*U. S. A.*

◇ ◇ ◇

First rat to get in haul in his tail.—*Virgin Islands.*

◇ ◇ ◇

Coward man keep soun' bone. (He who fights and runs away lives to fight another day.)—*Jamaica.*

◇ ◇ ◇

The house with an old grandparent harbors a jewel.—*Taiwan.*

◇ ◇ ◇

The more easily you get your wealth, the less good it will do you.—*Hebrew.*

◇ ◇ ◇